ScandinavianStitches

ScandinavianStitches

21 Playful Projects with Seasonal Flair

Kajsa Wikman

stashBOOKS

an imprint of C&T Publishing

Text and artwork copyright © 2010 by Kajsa Wikman

Artwork copyright © 2010 by C&T Publishing, Inc.

Publisher: Amy Marson

Creative Director: Gailen Runge

Acquisitions Editor: Susanne Woods

Editor: Lynn Koolish

Technical Editors: Ann Haley and Sandy Peterson

Copyeditor/Proofreader: Wordfirm Inc.

Cover/Book Designer: Kristy Zacharias

Production Coordinator: Kirstie L. Pettersen

Production Editor: Julia Cianci

Illustrator: Lon Eric Craven

Inspiration photography by Sanna Peurakoski, unless otherwise noted

Photography by Christina Carty-Francis and Diane Pedersen of C&T Publishing, Inc., unless otherwise noted

Published by Stash Books an imprint of C&T Publishing, Inc., P.O. Box 1456, Lafayette, CA 94549

Library of Congress Cataloging-in-Publication Data

Wikman, Kajsa.

Scandinavian stitches : 21 playful projects with seasonal flair / Kajsa Wikman.

p. cm.

ISBN 978-1-60705-007-0 (soft cover)

1. Patchwork--Patterns. 2. Quilting--Patterns. 3. Appliqué--Patterns. I. Title.

TT835.W53465 2010

746.46--dc22

2010006222

Printed in China

10 9 8 7 6 5 4 3 2

Dedication

For Elsa and Edvin, because you are the best!

Acknowledgments

Thank you to Susanne Woods for convincing me that it was the right time for me to write a book. Many thanks to everyone at C&T for helping me create a great book.

Thank you to Sanna for the amazing photography and the great teamwork.

Thanks to my immediate and extended family for the encouragement, the help, and the good laughs.

Hugs and kisses to Totte for the support through the ups and downs in the book-making process.

I would like to thank all my online friends for the encouragement you have given me through the years. Not a day passes by that I don't feel grateful that you found me and gave me your love. This book would not have been written without Laurraine, Jacquie, Amy, Alice, Katy, Mette, Anne, Di, Chara, Karen, Ruth, Lesley, Reetta, Mervi, Lucy, Anina, Marichelle, Ulla, Mirre, Agnes, Isabel, and many others.

Contents

Introduction

The first flowers of spring, the smell of the sea and fish, the warm colors of maple leaves…the different seasons here in Finland are very much connected to my creativity. Every season feels like a new beginning and above all like a good excuse to take on a new craft project. As I'm writing this, school will begin in two weeks, and even though it is still high summer, I am imagining the colorful leaves that will become the quilt you'll find on page 102.

Then the dark time will come, brightened up by the Yuletide season, which is the busiest time for my little business, with craft shows and social events, with candlelight, gingerbread, and mulled wine. And tomtar! More about them on pages 116–121. Then we wait and wait for the light and the snow and get cozy inside, maybe with some homemade buns and a new pillow (page 48). Your seasons might not be the same as mine, but I hope you enjoy looking into my world, finding inspiration, and learning something new. If you are new to sewing, I hope this book will encourage you to get started and find your own stitched path.

If it weren't for my children, I would probably still be looking for my deep artistic expression. Having children helped me realize that sometimes scratching the surface is enough to find your creative flow. Art can be playful and happy, and what could be more important than finding the simple joys in life?

I have found that my artistic mission is to make people smile. I hope this book will make you smile too.

THE ONLINE CRAFTING WORLD

In the early days of the Internet, there was a big fuss about all the opportunities it would bring. Not even in my wildest dreams did I ever imagine that I would be part of it in any way. I've never considered myself a computer nerd, but I've become one of the nerdiest moms on the street. I spent a lot of time online when I was at home with my babies, looking for a chance to talk about something other than diapers and baby food. What I found was a welcoming community of crafters and like-minded people. I discovered the blog world and started my own blog (http://syko.typepad.com), which has led to the creation of a network of friends around the globe.

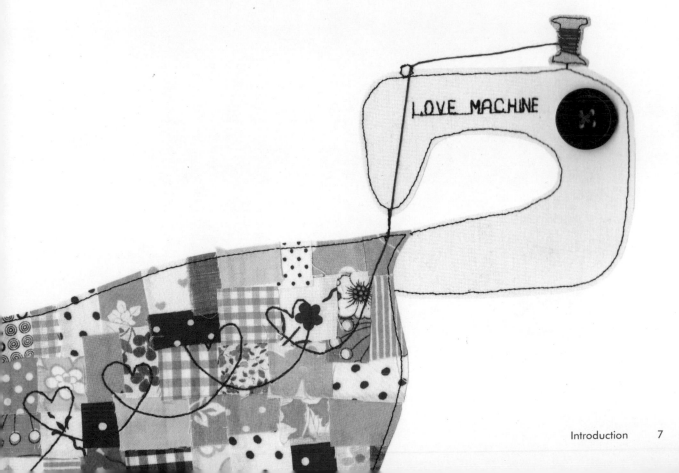

gettingstarted

BECOME INSPIRED

People often ask me where I get all my ideas. The short answer is that they just pop up. Still, the seed must have been planted at some point. The Internet is a great source of inspiration and is where I usually look first. Craft and design blogs, the photo-sharing community Flickr (flickr.com), and Etsy (etsy.com), an online marketplace for everything handmade, offer enough stimulation for a lifetime in front of the computer. The hardest thing is usually to turn off the computer and get started with your own projects.

The library is another source. My family and I are frequent patrons at the local library. Books and magazines provide a great excuse to take a refreshing break and have a few moments for yourself. How I love to sit down with a cup of tea and a magazine, surrounded by cozy pillows!

There is lots of inspiration to be found in illustrated children's books. The art in these books often has the playfulness I am looking for when I create my designs. I find it very rewarding to be able to read to my children and feed my creativity at the same time.

What originally led me to working with textiles was a love for traditional textiles and folk art. This was also what brought me to study ethnology and folklore at the university. I still find much inspiration from traditional textiles. An old tea towel with a beautiful hand-embroidered monogram that is too worn out to serve its original purpose can work very well as a base for a little art quilt. Traditional textiles are often simple, naive, and clever—exactly how I like my work to be.

An old tablecloth took on a new life in the shape of a bird.

I have had the advantage of growing up with the lovely, bold, and colorful designs by Finnish textile companies such as Marimekko, Nanso, and Finlayson, which are always an inspiration.

You never know when you might come across a new idea, so always have a notebook and a pencil or pen at hand. That is what I aim for. In real life I often end up scratching down my ideas on receipts from the supermarket, but any paper serves the purpose if the idea is good.

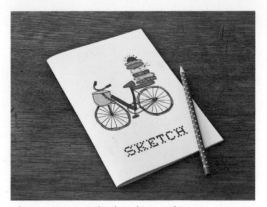
Always carry a notebook and a pencil or pen.

STAYING ORGANIZED

A simple—yet sometimes hard-to-follow—piece of advice is to organize your craft space. It is so much more inspiring to work when your table is empty, your fabrics are arranged by color, and your supplies are nicely organized in tins and jars. Thrift stores and yard sales are great places to find charming tins. And if you have a small craft space, don't collect fabrics and things you probably will not use anyway. Give them away and make room for the things you really like.

My sewing corner

Photo: Kajsa Wikman

PICKING THE RIGHT FABRICS

When I buy fabric I tend to be quite spontaneous. I have grown to trust my own taste. If I see something I like at a good price, I buy it because I know there will be a place to use it. Trust your instincts when you shop.

When you design a quilt or an appliqué piece, treat all your fabrics equally. Don't look at the designer's name on the selvage, and don't worry about whether the fabric is the latest trend or not. Focus instead on the color, print, and your vision of the design. In general, smaller prints tend to be more useful than bold prints, especially when used for appliqué, because the pieces you use are generally quite small. If you want the main focus to be on the appliqué, you don't want the prints on the fabrics to fight for attention.

After you have gone crazy shopping for your favorite prints, you will notice that you need to buy some plain solids too, because those are essential to make your favorite prints pop out from the quilt or pillow.

If the piece has a solid background in white, off-white, or black, you can use a lot of colors and prints in the details, and the result will still not look busy. Fabric with structure, such as natural linen or unbleached cotton, will make the background interesting but will not draw attention away from the main focus—the appliqué. You can also make the motif pop by quilting the background.

DESIGNING APPLIQUÉ

When I first tried appliqué, I searched in books and on the Internet for patterns. I couldn't find what I was looking for, so I decided to make patterns from my own drawings. I have never considered my drawing skills to be exceptional, but my naive style turned out to look surprisingly good translated into fabric and thread.

Try making your own appliqué patterns. Start out with something small, and allow yourself to experiment. Ask a child or a friend to draw a picture for you if you do not dare draw anything yourself. Children's drawings will often have the simplicity you are looking for. The birds that appear in many of my projects originated from a watercolor painting I did together with my daughter, Elsa, when she was four-years-old. We had read a very nice picture book and were inspired by a flock of birds on one page. I drew simple bird shapes that we colored with watercolors. Then I went away to take care of the laundry, and when I came back Elsa had given the birds the funniest beaks and legs!

Birds drawn by my daughter and me

If you feel that you don't have enough time for sewing, involve your children. Small children love to play with thread spools or sort buttons by color. While I was working on the autumn tree quilt on page 102, my seven-year-old daughter wanted to help. My first reaction was to say no, but I let her help me cut out some of the leaves. And, to use her words, all leaves do not look exactly the same in nature either. When we were finished cutting the leaves, she counted them: 52. Well done!

IT'S IN THE DETAILS

Tags and labels give your creation a finished look. You don't need fancy printed labels for this—I like to place lovely ribbons and trims in the seams. These make nice details and are great for placing a note to the receiver if you are making a gift.

Ribbons and trims make nice details for your sewing projects.

whatyou'llneed

TOOLS AND SUCH

To make the projects in this book, you will need some basic tools. The following are the tools I always have at hand when I work.

- Sewing thread, scissors, and a measuring tape
- Pins and a lovely pincushion (make one for yourself, page 27)
- A sewing machine that can sew straight and zigzag stitches. For free-motion stitching and quilting, you need to be able to drop or cover the feed dogs.
- For appliqué, a darning foot or an appliqué foot that either is transparent or has a wider opening in the front. For free-motion stitching, you'll need a quilting foot, a darning foot, or an embroidery foot.
- A rotary cutter, a cutting mat, and an acrylic ruler
- An iron and ironing board (A hot iron can do wonders for a wonky piece of appliqué.)
- Quilting pins, safety pins, and/or temporary fabric adhesive spray. I am totally dependent on fabric adhesive spray and only pin my quilts when I really need to. Temporary fabric adhesive is great for keeping the quilt sandwich together. In my experience, you can quilt a baby quilt without using a single pin. How great is that?
- An erasable fabric pen or pencil to mark stitching or quilting paths when necessary
- A sewing machine table (This is very useful for quilting.)

FABRICS

Quilt shops offer a wonderful treasure of quilting fabrics that are suitable for the projects in this book. However, I recommend trying out other fabrics too. I like browsing through thrift stores for fabrics. Retro and vintage fabrics make a nice addition to a project, and you can be certain that the final product will be unique. Make sure your vintage fabrics are 100% cotton or other natural fibers so they will last a long time and can be washed and pressed. Wash *all* your fabrics (new and old) in hot water, and then hang them out in the fresh air to dry. They are ready to be used.

THREE REASONS TO USE VINTAGE FABRIC

Tradition

Ecology

Uniqueness

linen: looking back

Linen was the most common material for clothing and home textiles in Scandinavia before cotton fabrics came with industrialization. I love to feel the connection with history when I use linen, but there is also an ecological aspect—it is a material that can be locally produced in northern Europe. It has a wonderful surface and a natural starch and shine, and I love the wrinkles. If you can't get your hands on nice linen or can't stand the wrinkles, you can use natural-colored cotton instead. Another ecological choice is bamboo fabric. I used a bamboo and cotton blend fabric for the backing of the tree quilt on page 102.

THREAD

For regular sewing, I use either good-quality cotton or polyester thread. For quilting and free-motion stitching, I use a slightly thicker thread or machine embroidery thread, such as a 30-weight, that is still easy to use in a regular sewing machine.

Polyester thread is easy to sew with because it is very durable. Cotton thread is a more natural and traditional choice, and it comes in lovely colors. Choose what works best for you.

sewingandquilting

APPLIQUÉ

If appliqué sounds difficult, don't worry—I'm going to show you an easy way to appliqué. I use a raw-edge technique with paper-backed fusible web.

WHAT YOU'LL NEED

Paper-backed fusible web (Any brand is fine.)

Pencil

Scissors

Sewing thread

Machine embroidery thread (30-weight)

Fabrics

Instructions

Pick one of the projects from the book to get started. After you have learned this method, you can easily turn any picture into an appliqué pattern. When you use paper-backed fusible web, you need to reverse the appliqué pieces onto the paper side of the web. I have helped you with that step for the book projects. When I reverse a picture I usually use a window, which is cheaper than using a light table, and you always have one at hand.

1. Trace the patterns with a pencil onto the paper side of the fusible web.

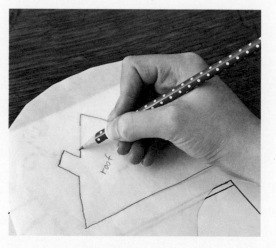

2. Roughly cut out the pieces with at least a ¼" (6mm) allowance. Place the pieces with the *paper side up* on the *wrong side of the fabric*, and press them using a dry iron.

3. Cut out the pieces on the drawn lines. Leave a ¼" (6mm) allowance wherever a piece will go underneath another piece. (This allowance is already added to the templates in this book.)

4. Peel off the paper, and place the pieces on the background fabric. The pieces with seam allowances should be placed under the pieces that overlap them. Press, fusing the appliqué pieces in place.

stitching down appliqués

I use black machine embroidery thread and a short straight stitch for most of my appliqués. I like the comic-like look the black outlines give the appliqués. If you don't stitch too close to the edges, the appliqués will survive in the washing machine, and only the outside edges will fray. If you don't want the appliqués to fray, hand washing is recommended. Stitching twice around the appliqués will make the edges more durable and is recommended for baby quilts or other items that require frequent machine washing. A tight zigzag stitch around the outside edges will prevent fraying, but it gives the appliqués a different look. The thread I use for the zigzag stitch is a little thicker than regular sewing machine thread, so it shows better, but still thin enough to work in a regular sewing machine without too much trouble.

NOTE

■ All appliqué patterns in this book are reversed for fusible web appliqué.

■ A $1/4''$ (6mm) seam allowance is included in all pattern pieces where required (when joined to another piece or overlapping another piece).

5. Thread your sewing machine with machine embroidery thread (cotton or polyester). Beginning with the pieces that are placed underneath, sew carefully around each motif with a short straight stitch.

6. Press from the wrong side.

FREE-MOTION STITCHING

When I talk about free-motion *stitching*, I refer to stitching freely on one layer of fabric; free-motion *quilting* is the same but through layers of fabric and batting.

Regular sewing machines usually have a darning foot with a circular opening. This foot is excellent to use for free-motion stitching. Some machines have other special feet for free-motion stitching. Setting your machine into a sewing table will enlarge your flat sewing area—this is helpful for free-motion stitching, as it is important to keep the fabric flat while you work.

Before you start stitching, you need to lower the feed dogs (refer to the machine manual if you don't know how to do this on your machine).

Now you will be able to move the fabric freely with your hands. Keep the fabric flat with your hands, and sew with a steady pace. Remember that your hands are replacing the feed dogs, so you have to guide the fabric yourself. Sew at different paces, first slowly and then faster, to find the speed that suits you and the project you are working on. If you do not get a good result, you might need to loosen the pressure on the presser foot or adjust the tension on the machine. It is also important to have a sharp needle. Choose a firm fabric when you first try free-motion stitching; it is easier to keep flat and wrinkle free.

Free-motion stitching is nice because of the personal handmade touch it provides. When I embroider script text with free-motion stitching, I begin by writing the text on the fabric freehand with an erasable fabric pen. When I sew, I use the prewritten text only as a guide. Don't start ripping and tearing if you don't follow the lines precisely—it probably doesn't matter.

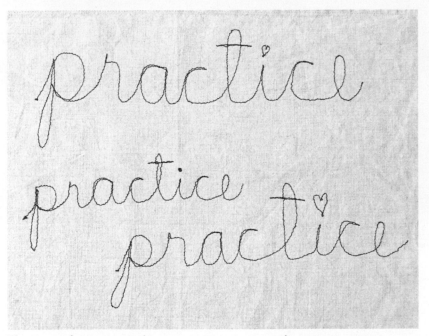

The secret to free-motion stitching is to practice, practice, and practice some more.

QUILTING

A quilt is assembled with three layers: the quilt top, the batting, and the backing. There is only one quilt with traditional piecing or patchwork in this book (*Frosty Baby Quilt*, page 32). The other quilts are made with appliqué quilt tops. I use low-loft cotton batting for the larger quilts, but you can use any batting you have at hand. Cotton is lovely because it is a natural and traditional material for quilts.

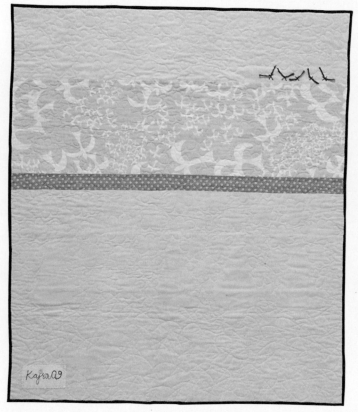

Improvised back of
Frosty Baby Quilt, page 32

Quilt Backing

I haven't provided any instructions for the quilt backings in this book. I usually use what I have left over from making the quilt top and put together a fairly improvised backing piece, and I encourage you to do the same. The quilt backing is a great place to be creative and try out new fabric combinations. Note that the backing and the batting should be slightly larger (1″–2″ larger on each side) than the quilt top when you start quilting.

Quilt Sandwich

Stacking and basting the quilt sandwich means putting together the layers: the quilt top, the batting, and the backing. To do this you'll need straight pins, safety pins, or temporary fabric adhesive spray.

I baste with temporary fabric adhesive spray, as explained on the following page. I work on the kitchen table or the floor, depending on how big my quilt is. You may want to cover the floor or table first to keep the overspray off the surface.

1. Place the batting down first, and place the backing right side up on top of the batting. Smooth out the backing.

2. Fold back half the backing, and spray the batting with temporary fabric adhesive on an area that is approximately 15″ (40cm) wide, parallel to the fold.

3. Unfold the fabric, and smooth it from the center toward the side. Continue in this manner until you have reached the edge of the quilt, and then do the same with the other half of the backing.

4. Turn the sandwich over, put the quilt top, right side up, on top of the batting, and smooth out the top.

5. Repeat Steps 1–4. Always work from the center to the edges.

If you get your quilt nice and smooth using the temporary fabric adhesive spray, you do not need to use many pins. For small quilts I usually do not use any pins at all with this method. Note that the adhesive is *temporary* and will not glue the fabrics together forever, so be sure you have time to quilt when you start making the sandwich.

If you are using pins to hold the quilt sandwich together, first arrange the layers—backing, batting, and quilt top—and work from the center of the quilt to make it nice and smooth, and then pin.

Layer the quilt sandwich.

Free-Motion Quilting

Free-motion quilting allows you to experiment freely. You can either make a continuous pattern (as on *Frosty Baby Quilt*, page 32) or sew unattached shapes. In the latter case you need to secure the thread at the beginning and end of each figure. Then move to the next shape, leaving a loose thread in between—the threads will be cut off when you are finished. I used this method on the fish quilt (page 88). Covering a whole area with freely quilted shapes, as with the fabric basket (page 40), is commonly called stippling.

There is no secret to free-motion stitching and quilting. The best advice is to practice, practice, and practice. I suggest you start with the pincushion project (page 27).

Binding

The last step in making a quilt is to sew on the binding. When you have finished quilting the quilt, trim the edges so that the batting and backing are the same size as the quilt top.

When I bind a quilt, I use the single-fold binding technique with mitered corners. I cut the binding fabrics crosswise to save fabric, but if you like you can cut them on the bias to give more stretch to the binding strips. For all the quilts in this book, I used 1″ (2.5cm) strips and a ¼″ (6mm) seam allowance. The binding is stitched to the back by hand.

The binding strips should be as long as the sum of all four edges of the quilt, plus at least 10 extra inches for the corners. If necessary, join several strips together. Place the strips together at a right angle, right sides facing. Stitch diagonally as shown. Trim the seam allowance, and press open.

1. Press the full strip in half lengthwise, and fold the edge on a short side. With a raw edge of the binding aligned with the edge of the quilt, start stitching from the middle on one edge, and sew until you are ¼″ (6mm) from the quilt corner.

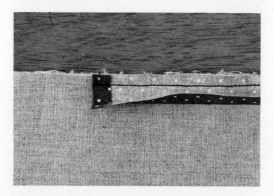

2. Remove the quilt from the sewing machine. Fold the binding up at a right angle, and then fold it straight down. It should be even with the edge of the quilt. Continue sewing, beginning ¼″ (6mm) from the edge of the quilt.

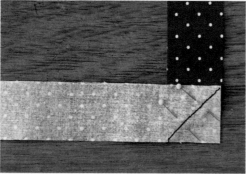

3. Repeat Steps 1–2 for the rest of the edges and the corners.

4. Fold the binding strip over the edges to the back of the quilt. Press. Fold in the seam allowance, and pin around the edges. Create diagonal folds at each corner. I usually pin as I go and create the corners when I reach them. I always stitch the binding to the back by hand. I find it

hard to get a neat look when stitching by machine, but it is worth a try!

EMBROIDERY

I like stitching on my machine, but some things I prefer to embroider by hand. For embroidering by hand you'll need embroidery floss and a needle. When I make the eyes and mouths for my tomte stuffies and fairy angels, I try to hide the knots inside them—otherwise, the thread is secured on the back side of the work. Sometimes it is better to show off a knot than try to hide it, as I've done on the back of *Frosty Baby Quilt* (page 22).

The hand embroidery stitches shown at right are used in this book.

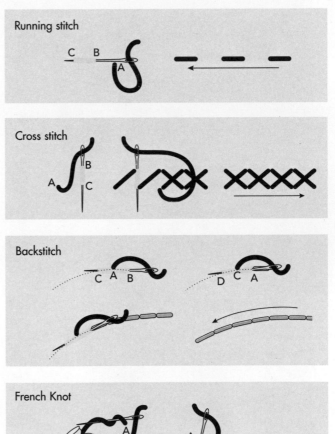

Running stitch

Cross stitch

Backstitch

French Knot

I JUST DON'T GET IT!

When you sew and craft, there are always moments of frustration, and ripping and redoing are part of the sewing process. The following are some typical problems and possible solutions.

PROBLEM: I just can't figure out this pattern!

SOLUTION: Take a break. Put the project aside, do something else, and get back to it later.

PROBLEM: I just keep making the same mistake over and over again!

SOLUTION: This is usually what happens when I am too tired. My best advice for you is to get some sleep. If that doesn't feel like a good solution, put the project aside, and come back to it later.

PROBLEM: I can't decide which fabrics to choose for my quilt!

SOLUTION: One tip is to hang the fabric options on the wall if you have a design/inspiration board; otherwise, place them on a table. Step back to look at them. Is there a fabric that stands out too much or has the wrong shade when looked at from a distance? Continue evaluating, adding and taking away fabrics until you are satisfied. Do try out fabrics that don't seem to fit in at first glance. If you just can't decide, I recommend that you sleep on it—leave the fabrics overnight, and take a fresh look at them the next day.

PROBLEM: Everything went wrong. I'm throwing it away!

SOLUTION: Put it aside instead; you might be able to save it. I have come up with many new ideas because of mistakes I've made.

PROBLEM: My quilting is a disaster!

SOLUTION: Try adjusting the presser-foot pressure or the tension, or put in a fresh, sharp needle. When you free-motion stitch it is important to have a sharp needle.

Most problems can be solved with a fresh perspective.

sew me a pincushion

This is a great first free-motion stitching project. I suggest that you cut out several patches of fabric and experiment with the free-motion script. If you end up with a number of nice pieces, you can make several pincushions or maybe use the patches for a quilt. Try stitching many different words.

Finished size: 5″ × 3″ (12.7cm × 7.6cm)

WHAT YOU'LL NEED

Fabrics
4″ × 5″ (10.2cm × 12.7cm) scrap of natural-colored linen or cotton

6″ × 6″ (15cm × 15cm) square of print fabric for back

3 scraps of cotton print for small patches

Notions and Supplies
Black 30-weight thread

Stuffing

Erasable fabric pen or pencil

3″ (7.6cm) length of ribbon

TIP

If you want a key ring instead of a pincushion, you can make a slightly smaller pillow and add a ring or natural twine to the short side.

CUTTING

Linen:
Cut 1 piece 3½″ × 4½″ (8.9cm × 11.4cm) for the front.

Print:
Cut 1 piece 3½″ × 5½″ (8.9cm × 14cm) for the back.

Print scraps:
Cut 3 squares 1½″ × 1½″ (3.8cm × 3.8cm).

INSTRUCTIONS

Seam allowances are ¼" (6mm) unless otherwise noted.

1. Set your sewing machine for free-motion stitching: lower the feed dogs, and attach the darning foot. Thread the machine with black thread.

2. Draw the script on the linen patches with an erasable fabric pen or pencil. I suggest that you use your own handwriting and try a variety of words to practice and find your own writing style.

3. Start stitching, keeping the fabric flat with your hands while slowly moving it forward. Stop and breathe! Then go on.

4. Using the project photo as a guide, sew the 3 small squares together. Press. Sew them to the linen patch. Press.

5. Place the unit from Step 4 right sides together with the backing piece. Fold the ribbon in half, and baste along the side seam, with the fold on the inside. Stitch around the edges, leaving an opening.

6. Turn the piece right side out, and stuff firmly. You will need a lot of stuffing for a pincushion; you don't want the needles to come through the cushion.

7. Stitch the gap closed by hand.

Start a new sewing project using your pincushion!

TIP

I suggest that you cut a number of pieces from the linen if you want to practice free-motion stitching. If you prefer to work with a larger piece of fabric that is easier to handle, mark the sewing area on the linen fabric with a pen, and cut it out when you have finished stitching the text.

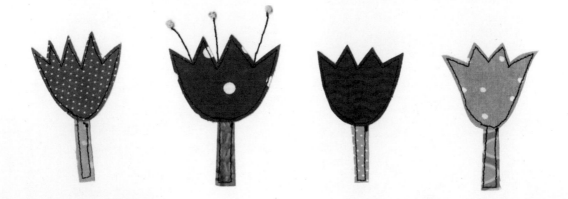

NATURSTIG
LUONTOPOLKU

winter

frosty baby quilt

It's January, and it's freezing outside. I look out the window over my desk and see a color combination that I would never have thought of. The icy weather and the long shadows make the snow turn light blue beside the spruces. A quilt is born! The fox is just my imagination…

This quilt has a lot of different fabrics but is easy and quite quick to assemble.

Finished size:
36″ × 42½″
(91.4cm × 108cm)

WHAT YOU'LL NEED

Fabrics

Note: A fat quarter is approximately 18″ × 22″ (46cm × 56cm).

A: ⅜ yard (35cm) or 1 fat quarter of blueberry blue

B: ⅜ yard (35cm) or 1 fat quarter of cloud blue

C: ⅜ yard (35cm) of light blue

D: ¼ yard (25cm) or 1 fat quarter of ice blue

E: 4″ × 4″ (10cm × 10cm) piece of blue with black print

F: ¼ yard (25cm) or 1 fat quarter of light blue polka dot

G: ½ yard (50cm) of sky blue

H: ¼ yard (25cm) or 1 fat quarter of light blue-and-white print

I: ⅓ yard (30cm) of white fabric

4 pieces 6″ × 8″ (15cm × 20cm) of different dark green solids for spruces

Scrap of dark brown fabric for tree trunks

Scrap of black fabric for birds

6″ × 10″ (15cm × 25cm) piece of bright orange fabric for fox

Scrap of off-white flannel for fox tail and bib

1½ yards (1.4m) of fabric for backing

¼ yard (25cm) of fabric for binding

Notions and Supplies

1½ yards (1.4m) of low-loft cotton batting

½ yard (50cm) of paper-backed fusible web

Black machine embroidery thread (30-weight)

Off-white machine embroidery thread (30-weight)

Skein of black embroidery floss

Fabric basting spray or quilting pins

CUTTING

Mark the blocks with their letters and numbers to help with placement (see Assembly diagram, page 35).

Blueberry blue:

A1: 6½″ × 7½″ (16.5cm × 19cm)

A11: 5″ × 13½″ (12.7cm × 32.4cm)

A15: 6″ × 15½″ (15.2cm × 39.4cm)

Cloud blue:

B2: 6½″ × 8½″ (16.5cm × 21.6cm)

B14: 6½″ × 18½″ (16.5cm × 47cm)

Light blue:

C3: 6½″ × 15″ (16.5cm × 38.1cm)

C13: 6½″ × 12″ (16.5cm × 30.5cm)

C19: 3½″ × 36″ (8.9cm × 91.4cm)

Ice blue:

D4: 6½″ × 6½″ (16.5cm × 16.5cm)

D5: 2½″ × 9½″ (6.4cm × 24.1cm)

D16: 6″ × 8″ (15.2cm × 20.3cm)

Blue with black print:

E6: 2½″ × 3″ (6.4cm × 7.6cm)

Light blue polka dot:

F7: 2½″ × 21″ (6.4cm × 53.3cm)

F12: 6½″ × 6½″ (16.5cm × 16.5cm)

Sky blue:

G8: 2½″ × 4″ (6.4cm × 10.2cm)

G9: 5″ × 16½″ (12.7cm × 41.9cm)

G18: 6½″ × 36″ (16.5cm × 91.4cm)

Light blue-and-white print:

H10: 5″ × 7″ (12.7cm × 17.8cm)

H17: 6″ × 13½″ (15.2cm × 34.3cm)

White:

I20: 9½″ × 36″ (24.1cm × 91.4cm)

Binding:

Cut 5 strips 1″ (2.5cm) wide × width of fabric (approximately 40″/102cm).

INSTRUCTIONS

Seam allowances are ¼" (6mm) unless otherwise noted. Press all the seams in the same direction when you assemble the strips.

1. Sew together the pieces as shown in the diagram: A1 + B2 + C3 + D4, D5 + E6 + F7 + G8, G9 + H10 + A11, F12 + C13 + B14, and A15 + D16 + H17. Sew G18 and C19 together lengthwise. Press all seams.

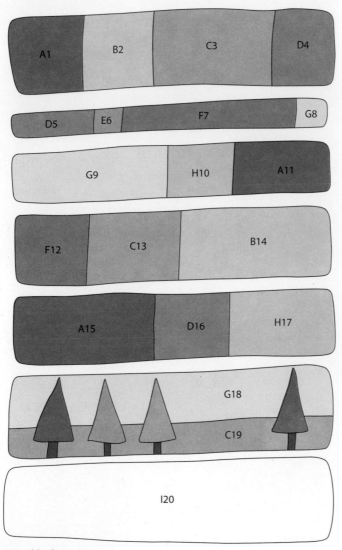

Assembly diagram

2. Prepare the appliqué pieces as described on pages 17–20. Trace the patterns (pages 38–39) onto the paper side of the fusible web, press it to the back of the fabrics, and cut out the shapes. Peel off the paper from the appliqué pieces, and fuse the trees onto the G18 + C19 strip, referring to the diagram (page 35).

3. Join the horizontal rows, and press.

4. Using the project photo as a guide, fuse the birds to the quilt top. Machine stitch around the edges of all the birds with a straight stitch using black embroidery thread. Add beaks and legs using a straight machine stitch, as shown on the bird pattern (page 39).

5. Fuse the fox appliqué to the white piece (snow). Machine stitch around the fox. Give the fox a mouth, and "tie" the bib with free-motion stitching (see photo below) or by hand with a backstitch using 2 strands of black embroidery floss. Stitch the eyes with French knots (page 25) using 6 strands of black embroidery floss.

6. Layer and baste the quilt layers together (pages 22–23).

7. Thread your sewing machine with off-white quilting thread, and set the machine for free-motion quilting. Stitch cloud shapes below through the layers all over the sky, starting from the middle of the quilt and stitch toward the edges. Quilt star shapes on the snow (page 39).

8. Join the 1″ binding strips to form a long strip (page 24). Fold the binding in half lengthwise with wrong sides together, and press. Attach the binding using the single-fold binding technique as described on pages 24–25.

TIP

Having a hard time finding enough blues for the background? Try the closet! Men's shirts are often made of good-quality cottons in nice blue shades that are great for quilts.

NOTE

Make 1 of each pattern unless otherwise noted. All patterns are reversed for fusible appliqué.

Cloud quilting pattern

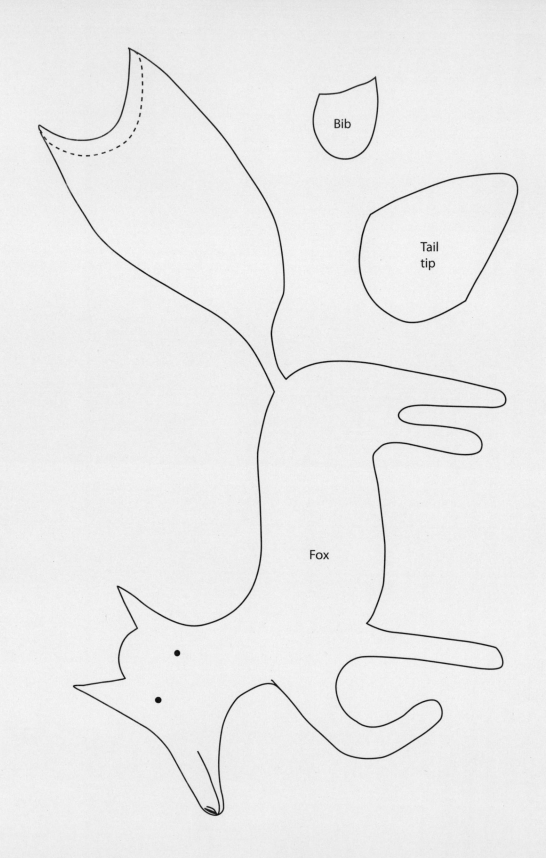

Bib

Tail
tip

Fox

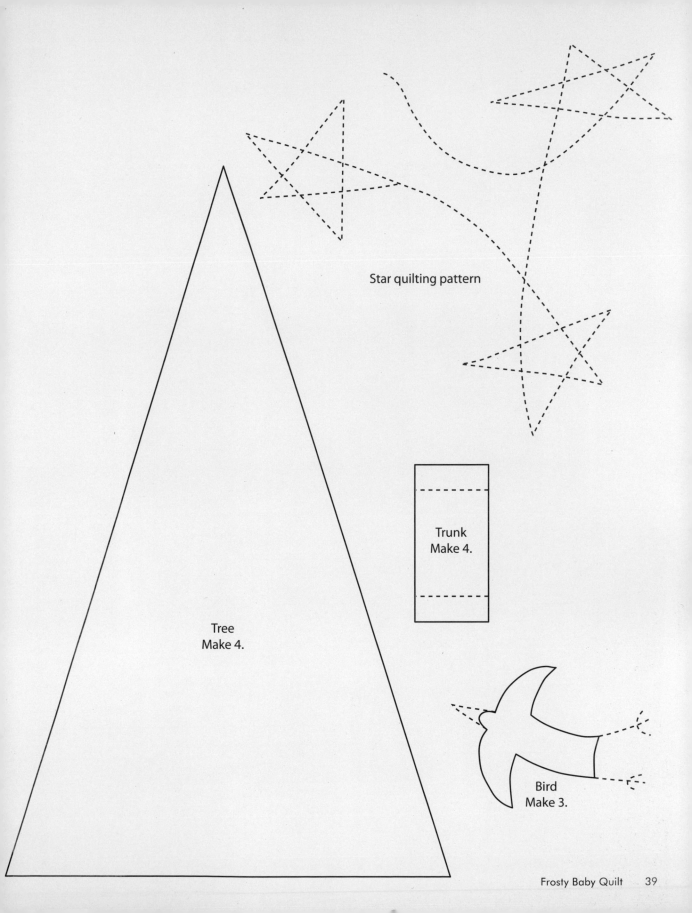

Star quilting pattern

Trunk
Make 4.

Tree
Make 4.

Bird
Make 3.

quilted basket

Socks, hats, scarves, and gloves are everywhere. Our entryway needs help—a quilted basket to hold everything is the solution.

This basket is made of five squares of the same size, so the measurements can easily be adjusted. Fat quarters are just the right size for the dimensions I chose. The quilting makes the basket quite sturdy, but you will need a metal wire for the upper edge—it is hidden by the folded top edge.

Finished size:
14½″ × 14½″ × 13½″
(37cm × 37cm × 34cm)

WHAT YOU'LL NEED

Note: A fat quarter is a quarter-yard of fabric cut 18″ × 22″ (approximately 46cm × 56cm).

Fabrics

Basket fabrics:

½ yard (45cm) or 1 fat quarter of light blue polka dot for side

1 yard (92cm) or 3 fat quarters of different light blue solids for sides

½ yard (45cm) or 1 fat quarter of light blue for bottom

½ yard (45cm) or 5 fat quarters of various red-and-white prints for lining

¼ yard (25cm) of red polka dot for binding

Appliqué fabrics:

¼ yard (25cm) or 1 fat quarter of red-and-white polka dot for socks appliqué

Scraps of red-and-white checkered fabric for sock tops and mitten and hat bands

Scraps of red-and-white fabric for mittens

Scrap of white fabric for cap

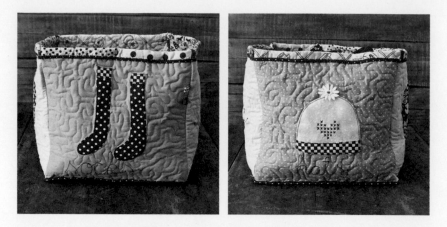

Notions and Supplies

1½ yards (122cm) of polyester batting 45″ (114cm) wide

½ yard (0.5m) of paper-backed fusible web

2 yards (2.0m) of bias tape to cover seams inside basket
   (I made my own bias tape from a red print.)

Black machine embroidery thread (30-weight)

Off-white machine quilting thread

Skein of red embroidery floss for hat

Temporary fabric adhesive spray or quilting pins

Flower or pom-pom to embellish hat

1¾ yards (1.6m) of wire for top of basket

CUTTING

Blue fabrics:
   Cut 5 squares 15″ × 15″
   (38cm × 38cm).

Red-and-white prints:
   Cut 5 squares 16″ × 16″
   (40.6cm × 40.6cm).

Red polka dot:
   Cut 4 strips 1″ (2.5cm) × width
   of fabric (approximately
   40″/102cm) for top and
   bottom binding.

Batting:
   Cut 5 squares 16″ × 16″
   (40.6cm × 40.6cm).

INSTRUCTIONS

Seam allowances are ¼" (6mm) unless otherwise noted.

1. Prepare the appliqué pieces as described on pages 17–20. Trace the patterns (pages 45–47) onto the paper side of the fusible web, fuse it to the wrong side of the fabrics, and cut out the shapes. Peel off the paper, and place the appliqués on the blue squares. Keep in mind that the upper edge of the basket will be folded about 1½" (4cm), and text will be added below the shapes.

2. Use an erasable fabric pen or pencil to write the script text below the appliqué pieces. The text patterns are on pages 45–47.

3. Transfer the cross-stitch heart to the cap. Stitch the cross stitches (page 45) using red embroidery floss.

4. Thread your sewing machine with black embroidery thread, and stitch around the edges of the appliqué pieces with a short straight stitch.

5. Set your sewing machine for free-motion stitching (pages 20–21), and stitch the text.

6. Layer and baste the 5 squares (pages 22–23). They will be joined after quilting.

7. Quilt the squares using off-white quilting thread. Trim the batting and backing even with the top fabric. Add a pom-pom to the top of the hat.

8. Stitch the 4 side squares together with right sides facing, covering the seams with bias tape as you go. To do this, stitch 2 squares together. Stitch the tape to one side, fold it over the seam allowance, pin it, and sew it down from the other side. Then add another side square, sew on the bias tape, and continue until you have formed the 4 sides of the basket, and all 4 seams inside the basket are covered with bias tape.

Bias tape covered inside seam

9. Stitch the bottom piece to the sides from the outside, wrong sides together. Sew 1 edge at a time. Keep your needle down at the corner point, pivot the basket, and sew to the next edge.

10. Join the 1″ (2.5cm) binding strips to form a long strip (page 24). Fold in half lengthwise with wrong sides together, and press. Stitch the binding to the top and bottom of the basket, enclosing the raw edges (pages 24–25).

11. Fold down the top edge of the basket about 1½″ (4cm), and place the wire inside. You can shape the basket to be either squared or round. Stitch the wire in place by hand with a few stitches on each side of the basket.

12. Throw your socks and mittens in your new basket!

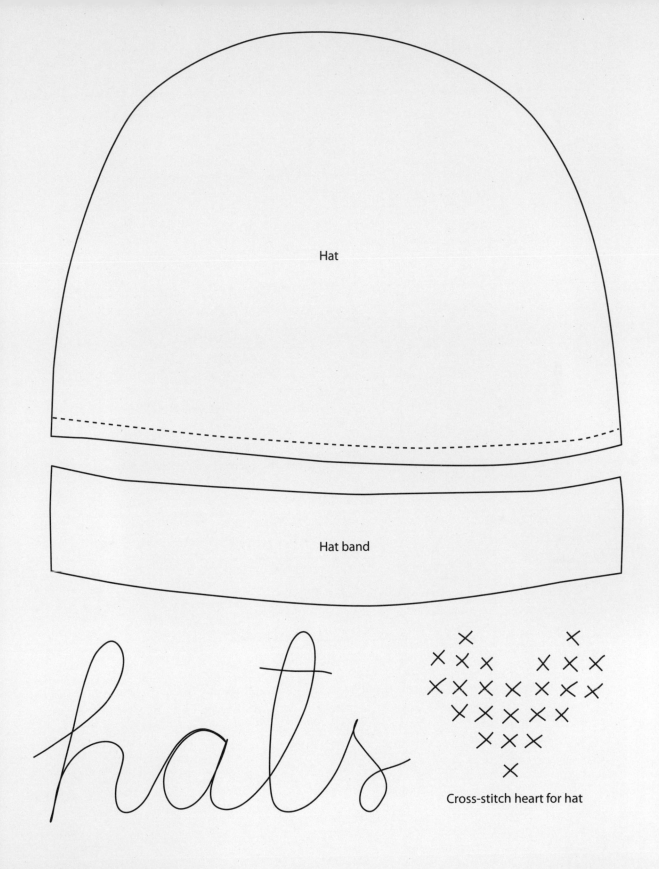

Hat

Hat band

hats

Cross-stitch heart for hat

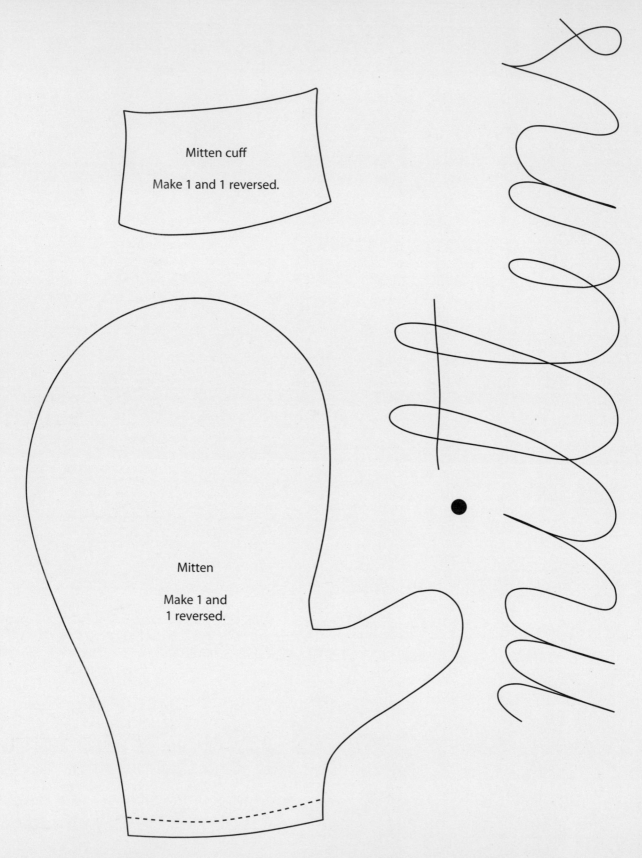

Mitten cuff

Make 1 and 1 reversed.

Mitten

Make 1 and
1 reversed.

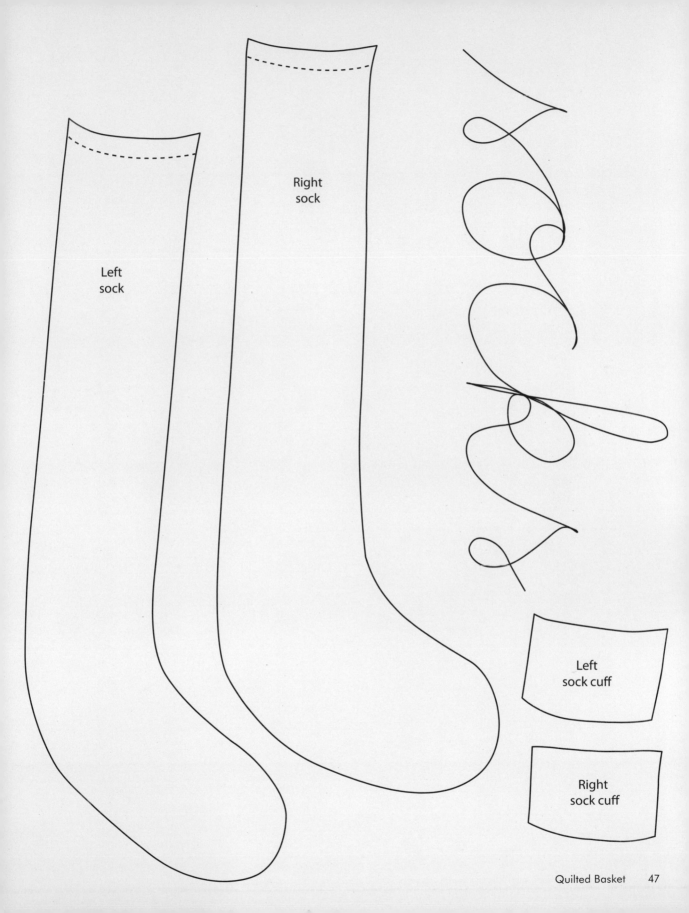

Left
sock

Right
sock

Left
sock cuff

Right
sock cuff

more tea? pillow

We've been out in the snow with our sleighs, and now we need something hot to drink to warm up our cold toes and something nice and sweet for our tummies.

This design can be varied very easily through the choice of fabrics and colors. My inspiration came from the vintage tablecloth I used for the teapot to give it a 1950s look. Use a blue-and-white toile de jouy print for the pot to create a different European look.

Finished size:
14″ × 14″
(35.6cm × 35.6cm)

WHAT YOU'LL NEED

Note: A fat quarter is a quarter-yard of fabric cut 18″ × 22″ (approximately 46cm × 56cm).

Fabrics

⅜ yard (35cm) or 1 fat quarter of natural-colored linen for background

⅜ yard (35cm) or 1 fat quarter of checkered fabric for pillow back

⅜ yard (35cm) or 1 fat quarter of white-and-red dotted fabric for back, teacup, and plate

¼ yard (25cm) of red-and-white gingham for tablecloth

10″ × 10″ (25cm × 25cm) teal print fabric for teapot

Scrap of white fabric for the inside of the teacup

Notions

¼ yard (25cm) of paper-backed fusible web

Black machine embroidery thread (30-weight)

Button for teapot

Button for closure on back

1 skein of black embroidery floss

Trim or lace for tags

14″ × 14″ 5.6cm × 35.6cm) for pillow form

CUTTING

Linen:

Cut 1 piece 9½″ × 14½″ (24.1cm × 36.8cm) for the background.

Checkered fabric:

Cut 1 piece 10″ × 14½″ (25.4cm × 36.8cm) for the back.

Red-and-white dotted fabric:

Cut 1 piece 10″ × 14½″ (25.4cm × 36.8cm) for the back.

Red-and-white gingham:

Cut 1 piece 5½″ × 14½″ (14cm × 36.8cm) for the tablecloth (Buy ½ yard [50cm], and cut it diagonally to do it my way).

INSTRUCTIONS

Seam allowances are ¼" (6mm) unless otherwise noted.

1. Place the linen and gingham right sides together, and stitch. Press the seam toward the darker fabric.

2. Prepare the appliqué pieces as described on pages 17–20. Trace the patterns (page 51) onto the paper side of the fusible web. Fuse it to the wrong side of the fabrics, and cut out the shapes.

3. Peel off the paper, and position the appliqués on the seamed fabrics. Don't place them too close to the edges of the pillow. Press them in place.

4. Thread your sewing machine with black thread. Sew with a short straight stitch around the edges of the pieces, starting with the piece placed underneath the cup.

5. Stitch the steam coming out of the teacup with 3 strands of black floss, using a running stitch (page 25). Sew a button on top of the teapot.

6. Now make the pillow back. Make a double 1" (2.5cm) fold to the wrong side, along one of the 14½" (36.8cm) edges of the checkered fabric. Press. Do the same for the dotted fabric. Sew down the folds by topstitching near the edge.

7. Make a buttonhole in the center of the folded edge of the checkered piece.

8. Stitch the trim or lace tabs to the left side of the pillow as shown in the project photo (page 48).

9. Place the pillow front face up. Overlap the back pieces, and place them face down on top of the pillow front so that the outside edges are aligned and the piece with the buttonhole is closest to the pillow front. Stitch the pillow front to the backs, and zigzag the raw edges.

10. Turn the pillow right side out, and sew on the button. Insert pillow form.

11. Have a tea party!

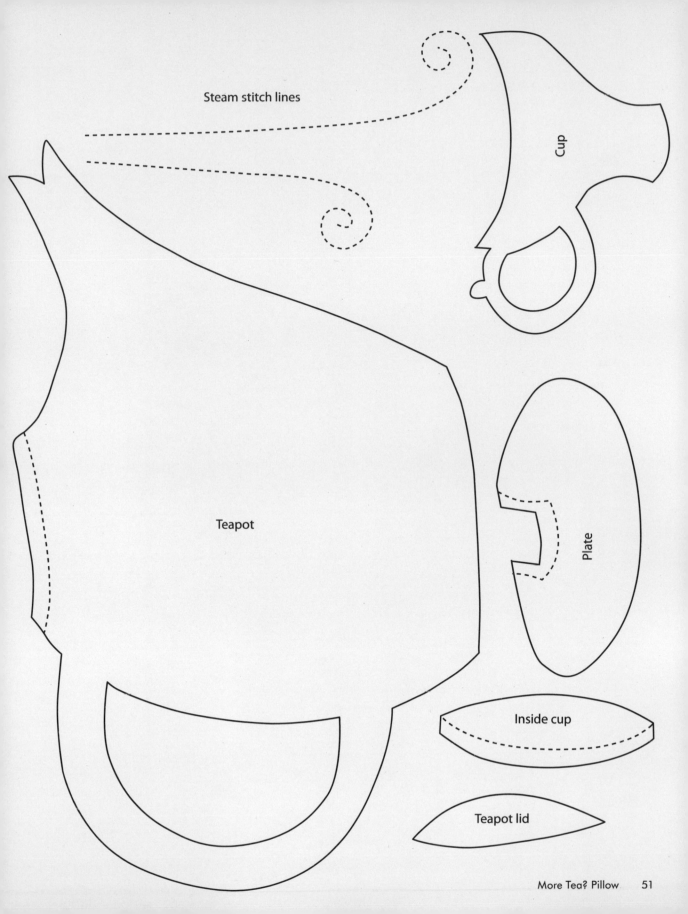

Steam stitch lines

Cup

Teapot

Plate

Inside cup

Teapot lid

spring

bird ornaments for easter

There still aren't many signs of spring, but Easter means that spring is on its way. We sow wheat seeds on a thin layer of soil on a plate or in a nice bowl and put branches in water, hoping for some early leaves.

Embroidered tablecloths that no longer serve their original purpose are great material for birds. The birds will not be washed, so it doesn't matter if the fabric is fragile and has a few small holes—it only adds to the charm

Finished size: approximately 5" (13cm) from beak to tail

WHAT YOU'LL NEED

Fabrics

8" × 8" (20cm × 20cm) of floral print fabric for bird body

Scrap of natural-colored linen for beak

3" × 20" (8cm × 50cm) strip of solid yellow or lime fabric for tail

Notions and Supplies

Natural twine and wooden beads for legs

Sequins and glass beads for eyes

Polyester stuffing

Pinking (zigzag) scissors

INSTRUCTIONS

Seam allowances are ¼″ (6mm) unless otherwise noted.

1. Cut 1 strip 1″ × 18″ (2.5cm × 46cm) long from the solid fabric for the tail, using pinking shears to prevent raveling. The bird can also be made without a tail.

2. Cut out the bird and beak pieces using the patterns below. Cut 2 of each (1 and 1 reversed).

3. Place the beak on the right side of the pattern piece, and stitch it to the body piece with a straight stitch, leaving a raw edge.

4. Make the legs by cutting 2 pieces of twine 3″ (8cm) long and tying a knot at one end of each piece. Thread the wooden beads on the twine. Stitch the legs to the edge of the body piece, referring to the marks on the pattern.

5. Place the body pieces right sides together, and stitch, leaving an opening at the tail. The legs should remain on the inside. Trim the seam allowances, clip curves as necessary, and turn right side out.

6. Stuff the bird. Fold the tail strip in fourths, stitch to secure the folds, and place in the opening. Pin the tail in place, and stitch the opening closed.

7. Make the eyes using sequins with glass beads in the middle; the beads will keep the sequins in place. Then add a hanging loop, and your birdie is ready to leave the nest!

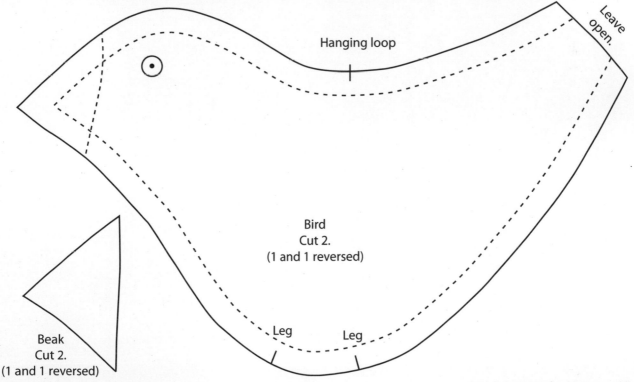

Hanging loop

Leave open.

Bird
Cut 2.
(1 and 1 reversed)

Leg   Leg

Beak
Cut 2.
(1 and 1 reversed)

bird nest quilted bowl

There was a terrible twitter in our kitchen. After some investigation, we found out that a family of sparrows had moved into a ventilation pipe underneath our window. They can stay. It won't take long until the babies fly out of the nest anyway.

This is a nice weekend project, and a fabric bowl filled with goodies is an appreciated gift. The pieces are quilted before the bowl is put together, and they are quite small and easy to work with, so this is a great project if you are new to quilting.

Finished size:
approximately
6¼″ × 4½″
(15.9cm × 11.5cm)

WHAT YOU'LL NEED

Fabrics

¼ yard (25cm) of linen for bowl

⅜ yard (35cm) floral print fabric for lining and binding

4″ × 4″ (10cm × 10cm) piece of aqua polka dot fabric for bird appliqué

Notions

4″ × 4″ (10cm × 10cm) piece of paper-backed fusible web

⅜ yard (35cm) polyester batting

White machine quilting thread

Black machine embroidery thread

Temporary fabric adhesive spray or quilting pins

Bright pink embroidery floss

Glass beads for bird eyes

CUTTING

Linen:

Cut 1 circle 6¾″ (17.1cm) in diameter.

Cut 1 strip 5″ × 21¾″ (12.7cm × 55.2cm).

Floral print:

Cut 2 strips 1″ (2.5cm) wide × width of fabric (approximately 40″/102cm) of the lining fabric for the binding.

Cut 1 circle 8¾″ (22.2cm) in diameter for the bottom.

Cut 1 strip 7″ × 23″ (17.8cm × 58.4cm).

Batting:

Cut 1 circle 8¾″ (22.2cm) in diameter.

Cut 1 strip 7″ × 23″ (17.8cm × 58.4cm).

INSTRUCTIONS

Seam allowances are ¼" (6mm) unless otherwise noted.

1. Prepare the bird appliqué as described on pages 17–20. Trace the pattern on page 59 onto the paper side of the fusible web, press it to the wrong side of the fabric, and cut out the shape. Place the bird on the linen strip, and fuse the bird in place.

2. To make the bottom of the bowl, make a quilt sandwich (pages 22–23) of the linen, batting, and lining. Pin or use fabric adhesive to keep the layers in place.

3. Set your sewing machine for free-motion quilting (page 23). Machine quilt the bowl bottom from the linen side using white quilting thread. A meandering stipple stitch pattern works well. (The project photo on page 56 shows a stipple quilting stitch pattern on the bowl's side.) Then trim the extra lining and batting even with the edge of the linen.

4. Make a quilt sandwich of the side strips. Using black quilting thread, appliqué the bird through the layers, adding the beak, the legs, and a tasty worm while sewing.

5. To make the bird nest, set your machine for free-motion stitching, and thread the machine with black quilting thread. Stitch back and forth to form a nest that is 3.5" (9cm) wide. Form 4 small heads and beaks on top of the nest.

6. Stipple quilt the rest of the side strip using white quilting thread, beginning from the middle of the piece.

7. Now let the mother bird fly to her small ones. Using 3 strands of pink embroidery floss, stitch the flying track by hand as shown in the illustration on page 59. Trim backing and batting to the same size as the top.

8. Give the little birdies small glass beads for eyes.

9. Fold and press the 1″ (2.5cm) strips to form binding.

10. To create a tube of the side piece, place the short ends right sides together. Pin and sew the side seam. You can bind the side seam for a nicer appearance as I did in the Quilted Basket (page 44). Bind the top edge with the 1″ (2.5cm) binding strip (pages 24–25).

11. Pin the bottom circle to the tube. Stitch the pieces together from the right side; the seam will be covered by the binding.

12. Stitch the binding on the linen side by the bottom of the bowl. Then hand stitch to fasten the other side of the binding.

13. Fill your bowl with goodies or the Easter bird ornaments!

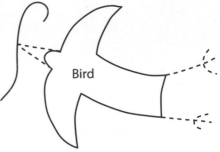

Bird

13 birds mini art quilt

Spring is here! The cold and wet weather is finally over, and the skies are filled with birds returning from their winter holidays. This little quilt is based on a watercolor painting I did with my daughter (page 12).

Finished size:
12½" × 9½"
(31.7cm × 24.1cm)

WHAT YOU'LL NEED

Fabrics

10" × 13" (25cm × 33cm) piece of white cotton or linen

14" × 17" (36cm × 43cm) piece of fabric for backing

Scraps of cotton for birds

Notions

14" × 17" (36cm × 43cm) piece of batting

10" × 13" (25cm × 33cm) piece of paper-backed fusible web

Black machine embroidery thread (30-weight)

White machine quilting thread

Temporary fabric adhesive spray or quilting pins

2" (5cm) piece of ribbon or trim (optional)

Button for trim (optional)

2 buttons for hanging

INSTRUCTIONS

Seam allowances are ¼" (6mm) unless otherwise noted.

1. Prepare the appliqué pieces as described on pages 17–20. Trace the patterns (page 63) onto the paper side of the fusible web, cut apart, press it to the fabric scraps, and cut out the shapes.

2. Arrange the birds on the fabric, keeping the outer seam allowances in mind.

3. Peel off the paper from the appliqué pieces, and fuse them to the background.

4. Machine stitch around the edges of all the birds with a straight stitch, using black embroidery thread. Sew the beaks and the legs on the birds at the same time. Refer to the project photo (page 60) and the bird pattern (page 59) to get some ideas for how to stitch the birds' legs and beaks.

5. If you want to add trim, now is the time to attach a button to a 2″ (5cm) piece of ribbon or trim. Fold the ribbon or trim, and baste it in place on the seam allowance on the left side of the background fabric.

6. Attach the little quilt top to the batting with fabric adhesive. Place the backing on the quilt top, right sides together. Sew around the edges, leaving an opening. Trim the batting and backing even with the quilt top on all sides. Turn the quilt right side out, and press from the back. Hand stitch the opening closed.

7. Thread your sewing machine with white quilting thread, and set the machine for free-motion quilting. Starting from the middle of the quilt, quilt the background, leaving the birds unquilted.

8. To make a hanging loop on the back, sew on 2 buttons and run a thread, like a figure-8, around and between them. The quilt is ready to hang.

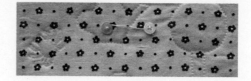

gardening angel

When the weather is wet and damp, and summer is too far away, I drag home piles of gardening books from the library to escape to warmer times. My gardening angel keeps me company and tells me that even if it's hopelessly gray today, there will be flowers one day. Check out her Yule sisters on page 126.

Finished size: approximately 9" (23cm) from tip to toe

WHAT YOU'LL NEED

Fabrics

¼ yard (25cm) of white fabric for dress

Scrap of off-white flannel for head

Scrap of red-and-white jersey knit for arms and legs

Scrap of red polka dot for watering can

9" × 14" (23cm × 36cm) of yellow tulle for wings

Notions and Supplies

Scrap of paper-backed fusible web

Machine embroidery thread (30-weight) in 2 shades of green for grass

Black machine embroidery thread (30-weight) for appliqué

Blue embroidery floss for water

Red thread for mouth

Linen yarn for hair

Tiny glass beads for eyes

Stuffing

TIP

Use jersey knit for the tiny arms and legs—the stretchy fabric makes them so much easier to work with.

INSTRUCTIONS

Seam allowances are ¼" (6mm) unless otherwise noted. Seam allowances are included in all pattern pieces, except the watering can.

1. Create templates for the dress, head, legs, and arms using the patterns (page 67). Trace the templates onto fabric, and cut out the pieces.

2. Place the head and dress pieces right sides together. Sew each pair together at the neck, and then press.

3. Prepare the watering can appliqué piece as described on pages 17–20. Trace the pattern (page 67) onto the paper side of the fusible web, press it to the fabric, and cut out the shape.

4. Fuse the appliqué piece to the front of the angel, and machine stitch around the edges with black thread.

5. Set your sewing machine for free-motion stitching (pages 20–21). Machine stitch the grass back and forth with a short straight stitch using the green machine embroidery threads. Start sewing with one of the threads from the bottom of the dress, and stitch grass blades of different lengths. Now switch to the other green thread, and sew more grass on top of the previous stitching.

6. Hand stitch the water coming out of the watering can with 3 strands of blue embroidery floss using a running stitch (page 25).

7. Wrap linen yarn around 3 of your fingers until it is thick enough for the angel's hair. Stitch it to the head within the seam allowance. Sew back and forth several times by machine to keep the hair in place. Give the angel a face using black beads and 2 strands of red embroidery floss.

Stitch back and forth

8. Place the arm pieces right sides together. Stitch them, turn them right side out, and stuff with stuffing. Repeat for the legs. Stitch the arms and legs to the dress where indicated on the pattern.

9. Pin the angel pieces right sides together. Make sure that the arms and legs are on the inside. Stitch, leaving an opening in the side.

10. Turn the angel right side out, and stuff with stuffing. Hand stitch the gap closed.

11. Fold the tulle in half so it measures 9" × 7" (23cm × 18cm). Sew down the middle with long stitches, pull the thread to gather the stitches, and hand stitch the wings to the back of the angel. Cut the wings to a nice round shape as shown in the project photo (page 64).

12. Make a hanging loop by taking a small stitch with a needle and thread through the middle of the head and knotting the ends. Cut her hair, and she's ready to fly!

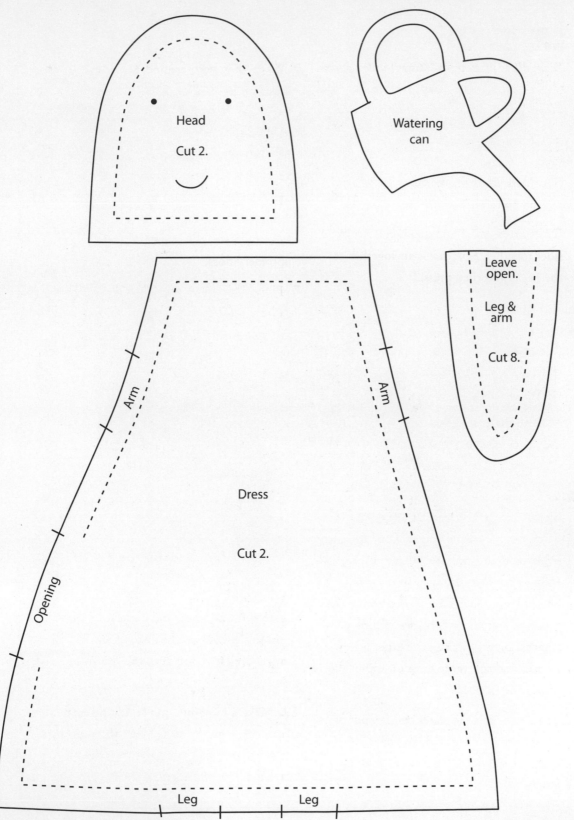

Head

Cut 2.

Watering can

Leave open.

Leg & arm

Cut 8.

Dress

Cut 2.

Arm

Arm

Opening

Leg

Leg

garden shed

A gardening angel has to have somewhere to put all her tools. This also makes a nice little housewarming gift—just swap out the window for a house number.

Finished size: approximately 3″ × 7½″ (8cm × 19cm)

Fabrics

¼ yard (25cm) of red polka dot for house

5″ × 10″ (13cm × 25cm) piece of floral print for roof

Fabric scraps for door and window

Notions

Paper-backed fusible web

Black machine quilting thread

Button for doorknob

Trim for chimney

Stuffing

Thread for hanging

See the Yule House Ornament project (pages 122–125) for sewing instructions and patterns.

1 caught a fish alive

six seven eight nine

then 1 let go ago

why did you let it

use it bit my finger

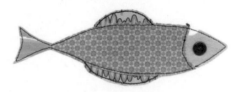

summer

on the road pillow

The first warm summer weekends in June, the roads are crowded with cars full of families rushing to their summer houses in the countryside and by the sea.

If you like to arrange many pieces, this project is for you! If you feel really inspired, you can add an embroidered cloud (page 37) with backstitch and maybe a few tulips (page 126) to the design.

Finished size:

16" × 16"

(40.6cm × 40.6cm)

Fabrics

½ yard (50cm) of white linen or cotton for background

½ yard (50cm) of polka dot cotton in black and white for back

⅜ yard (35cm) or 1 fat quarter 18" × 22" (46cm × 56cm) of black fabric for road

Fabric scraps for small appliqués

Notions

½ yard (50cm) of paper-backed fusible web

Black machine embroidery thread (30-weight)

4 buttons for car wheels

Black glass bead for horse eye

Linen yarn for horse mane and tail

Lime green embroidery floss for grass

White embroidery floss for road marks

3" (8cm) piece of trim for tag

2 white buttons for pillow closure

16" × 16" (40.6cm × 40.6cm) pillow form

White fabric:

Cut 1 square 16″ × 16″ (40.6cm × 40.6cm) for the front.

Black Polka dot fabric:

Cut 2 pieces 11″ × 16″ (28cm × 40.6cm) for the back.

TIP

Factory-made pillow inserts tend to be a bit loose in structure, so don't add seam allowances. This way the cover will sit nice and tight.

INSTRUCTIONS

1. Trace the appliqué templates (pages 76–77) onto the paper side of the fusible web, and roughly cut them out. Fuse the roughly cut shapes onto the scraps, and cut out on the lines.

2. Peel off the paper from the prepared fabric pieces, and place on the background. Make sure that the pieces with seam allowances are placed under the top pieces. Use the pattern and project photo for reference.

Fuse the road into place bit by bit, starting at one end and adding the other items as you go on. Note that the horse should be fused only by the legs at first!

3. Now make the horse mane and tail by rolling the linen yarn around 2 fingers a few times. Lift the horse, insert the tail into its place, and stitch it to the background fabric under the horse. Do the same with the mane. Fuse the horse in place.

4. Thread your machine with black machine embroidery thread, and stitch around the horse. Trim the mane and tail.

5. Set your machine for free-motion stitching, and "write" the shop text and the clock face. You might need to practice on a scrap first!

6. Appliqué the remaining pieces with a straight machine stitch and black machine embroidery thread.

7. Stitch the lines on the road with 4 strands of white embroidery floss using a running stitch. Give the horse some grass using a backstitch (page 25) and 2 strands of lime green floss. Then sew the button wheels on the cars.

8. Now make the back. Make a double 1″ (2.5cm) fold along the long edge of one of the back pieces. Press. Double fold one long edge of the other back piece ½″ (1.3cm), and press. Stitch.

9. Make 2 buttonholes on the back piece with the wider fold.

10. Stitch the trim tag to the left seam allowance of the pillow front.

11. Place the back pieces with their right sides facing the front piece. Overlap the back pieces so the piece with the buttonholes is closest to the front piece. Stitch and zigzag the raw edges, leaving an opening for turning. Turn right side out, and sew on the buttons. Insert pillow form.

12. Hit the road!

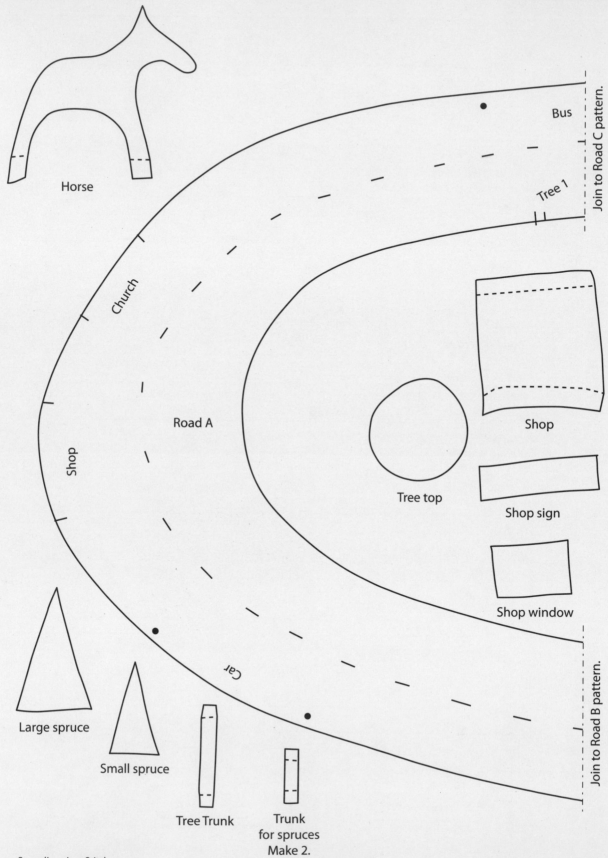

Horse

Bus

Join to Road C pattern.

Tree 1

Church

Road A

Shop

Tree top

Shop

Shop sign

Shop window

Join to Road B pattern.

Car

Large spruce

Small spruce

Tree Trunk

Trunk
for spruces
Make 2.

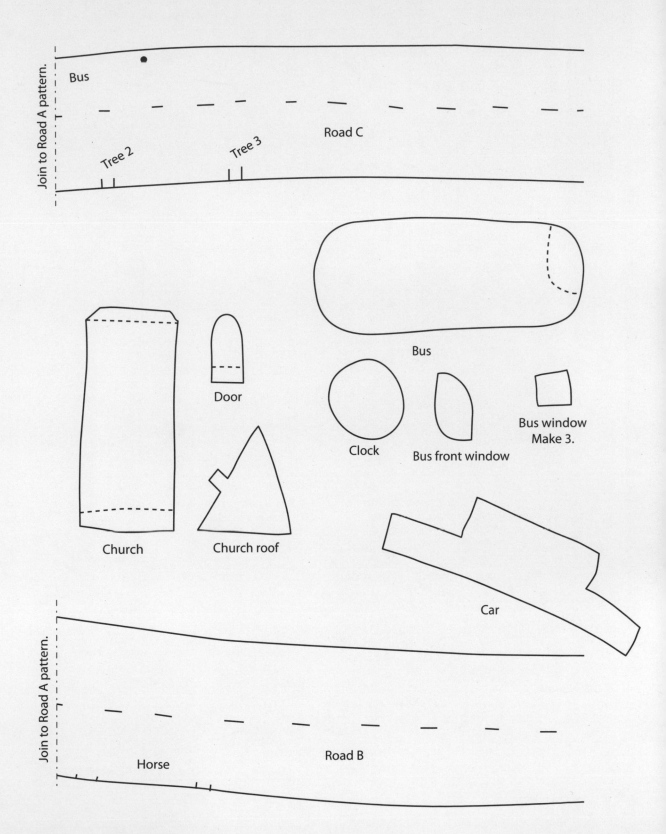

Bus

Join to Road A pattern.

Road C

Tree 2

Tree 3

Door

Bus

Clock

Bus front window

Bus window
Make 3.

Church

Church roof

Car

Join to Road A pattern.

Horse

Road B

at the summer house

A red wooden house by a lake surrounded by birch trees—that's what most Finns long for during the dark winter days. And when summer comes, many people live out their dream of the simple life!

This project is easy to accomplish if you are a beginning quilter. It has no batting or binding and is quilted only around the appliquéd shapes. I chose this method to make the piece easy to slip into a store-bought frame. The size can be adjusted to fit a frame with different measurements than mine—just add fabric around the appliqué design!

Finished size:
approximately
11″ × 8½″
(28cm × 22cm)
including frame

Size of appliqué:
approximately
10″ × 7″
(28cm × 18cm)

WHAT YOU'LL NEED

Fabrics

14″ × 10″ (36cm × 25cm) piece of white cotton (or enough to fit your frame) for background

14″ × 10″ (36cm × 25cm) piece of fabric for backing

6½″ × 6½″ (16.5cm × 16.5cm) piece of red polka dot fabric for house

6½″ × 5″ (16.5cm × 13cm) scrap of black-and-white fabric for roof

Scrap of lime print fabric for birch tree

Scrap of white-and-black fabric for tree trunk

Scrap of lime fabric for door

Scraps of white and aqua fabric for window

Fabric scraps for clothes

Notions

14″ × 10″ (36cm × 25cm) piece of paper-backed fusible web

Black machine embroidery thread (30-weight)

White machine embroidery thread (30-weight)

Black embroidery floss for smoke

Red embroidery floss for pegs (clothespins)

Mother-of-pearl button for doorknob

Fine-point black permanent marker

Picture frame approximately 8″ × 10″ (20cm × 25cm) or 8½″ × 11″ (22cm × 28cm)

INSTRUCTIONS

Seam allowances are ¼" (6mm) unless otherwise noted.

1. Trace the appliqué patterns (pages 80–81) onto the paper side of the fusible web, cut them out, and fuse them onto the fabric scraps. See pages 17–20 for more tips on fusible appliqué.

2. Peel off the paper from the prepared fabric pieces, and arrange them on the background fabric. *The pieces with seam allowances marked are placed underneath.* Use the project photo for reference. Mark the clothesline with a permanent marker. The clothes are placed ¼" (6mm) beneath.

3. Fuse the pieces to the background.

4. Machine stitch around the edges of all the appliqué pieces with a straight stitch, using black machine embroidery thread. Sew the clothesline next, back and forth with 2 lines of stitching, one on top of the other.

5. Stitch the smoke coming out of the chimney with 4 strands of black embroidery floss using a running stitch. Sew the clothespins with 4 strands of red floss. Attach the button for the doorknob with the same floss.

6. Trim the edges of the front and back pieces to 11½" × 9" (29.2cm × 22.3m) or to fit your frame.

7. Stitch the front and back pieces together with right sides facing, using a ¼" (6mm) seam allowance and leaving an opening. Turn the quilt right side out, and press from the back. Hand stitch the gap closed.

8. Thread your sewing machine with white quilting thread, and stitch carefully around the appliquéd motifs.

9. Press from the back, and slip into your frame!

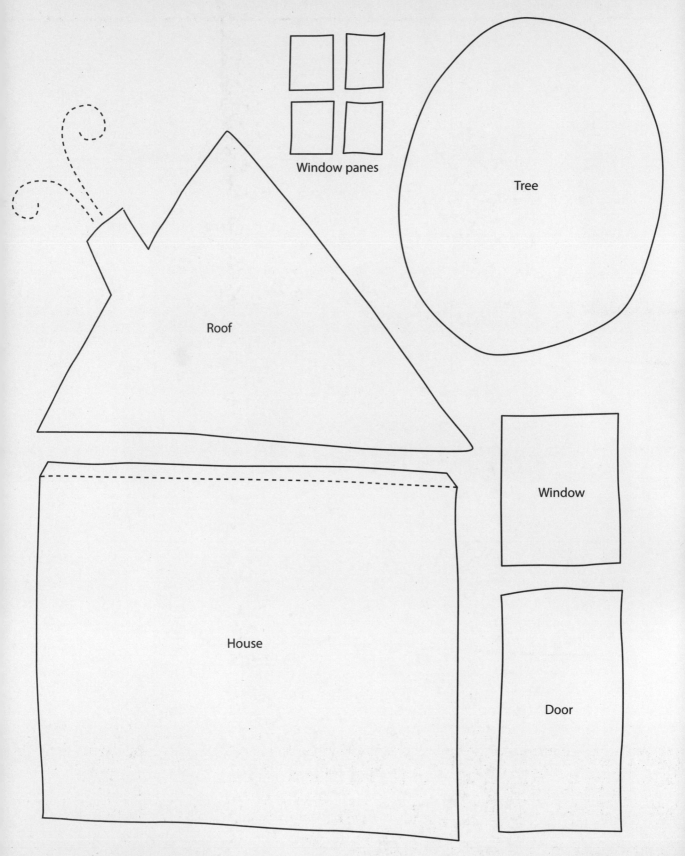

Window panes

Tree

Roof

Window

House

Door

silakka = finnish for "herring"

silakka pillow

Baltic herring? They are the little fish swimming around our coasts, and they are a cornerstone in the traditional Finnish kitchen. On Midsummer's Eve, herring is consumed together with new potatoes and dill. The inspiration for the simple fish shapes used in this pillow comes from Scandinavian textiles from the 1950s and '60s. The next project also features another tasty fish friend.

Finished size:
16″ × 16″
(40.6cm × 40.6cm)

WHAT YOU'LL NEED

Fabrics

½ yard (50cm) of natural unbleached linen for background

½ yard (50cm) of polka dot cotton in white and teal for back

10 scraps of teal and lime fabrics for herring appliqués

4 scraps of black-and-white fabric for fish appliqués

Notions

¼ yard (25cm) of paper-backed fusible web

Black machine embroidery thread (30-weight)

4 buttons for fish eyes

3″ (8cm) piece of trim for tag

Large button for pillow closure

16″ × 16″ (40.6cm × 40.6cm) pillow form

INSTRUCTIONS

Seam allowances are ¼" (6mm) unless otherwise noted.

TIP

Not crazy about herring? Try with another text. How does "school" sound?

1. Cut 1 square 16" × 16" (40.6cm × 40.6cm) from the linen for the front piece of the pillow. Cut 2 pieces from the polka dot fabric each measuring 11" × 16" (28cm × 40.6cm) for the back.

2. Trace the fish (patterns are on pages 85–86) onto the paper side of the fusible web, cut out, and fuse onto the fabric scraps. See pages 17–20 for more tips on fusible appliqué.

3. Peel off the paper from the prepared fabric pieces, and place on the background. Make sure the pieces with seam allowances (shown with dashed lines) are placed under the top pieces. Use the project photo for reference as you place the appliqué pieces in the numbered order. Remember to leave room for the text beneath the fish! Be sure not to place them too close to the edges, as the round shape of the pillow insert will then hide them.

4. Use an erasable fabric pen to prewrite the text. You'll find my text on page 87, but your own handwriting will make it more personal. Thread your machine with black machine embroidery thread. Set your sewing machine for free-motion quilting, and start writing!

5. Now make the back. Make a double 1" (2.5cm) fold along the long edge of one of the back pieces. Press. Double fold the long edge of the other back piece ½" (1.3cm), and press. Stitch.

6. Make a buttonhole in the middle of the back piece with the wider fold.

7. Stitch the trim to the left side of the pillow.

8. Place the back pieces on the front piece, with the piece with the buttonhole closest to the front piece. The back pieces should overlap by 3", and their right sides should be against the front right side. Stitch and zigzag the raw edges. Turn right sides out, and sew on the button.

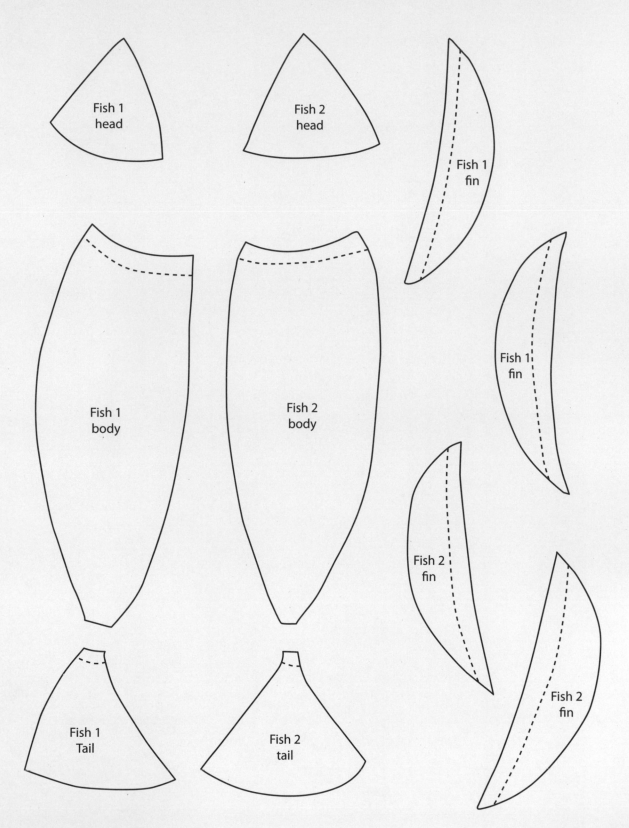

Fish 1 head

Fish 2 head

Fish 1 fin

Fish 1 fin

Fish 1 body

Fish 2 body

Fish 2 fin

Fish 1 Tail

Fish 2 tail

Fish 2 fin

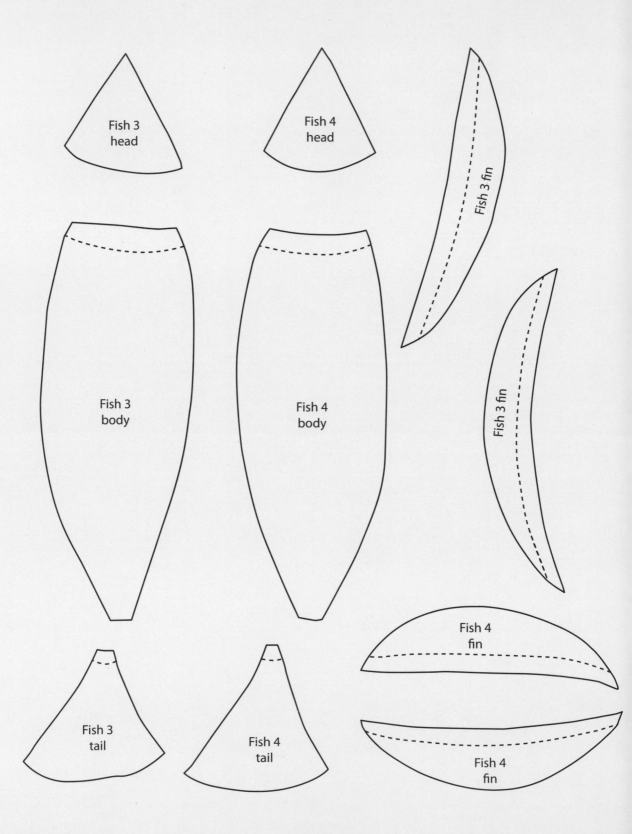

Fish 3
head

Fish 4
head

Fish 3 fin

Fish 3 fin

Fish 3
body

Fish 4
body

Fish 4
fin

Fish 3
tail

Fish 4
tail

Fish 4
fin

one two three four five
once I caught a fish alive
six seven eight nine ten
then I let go again
why did you let it go
because it bit my finger so
which finger did it
bite this little finger on the right

once i caught a fish quilt

We are on holiday by the sea. A seagull woke me up, and I am now sitting all by myself on a cliff watching the horizon, listening to the waves, and feeling the fresh breeze in my hair. I want this moment to last forever. Maybe I can catch it in a quilt when I get home.

There is no traditional piecing involved in this quilt. If you have some experience in free-motion quilting, this will be a nice weekend project.

Finished size: 41″ × 44″ (104.1cm × 111.8cm)

WHAT YOU'LL NEED

Fabrics
Fabric width at least 44" (111.8cm)

1½ yards (1.5m) of natural-colored linen or cotton for background

1½ yards (1.5m) of cotton print(s) for backing

¼ yard (25cm) of black-and-white striped cotton for binding

Scraps of 12 different black-and-white fabrics for herring appliqué

Scraps of 4 different brown prints for flounder appliqué

Scrap of off-white felt for flounder eyes

Notions

1½ yards (1.5m) of low-loft cotton batting

½ yard (50cm) of paper-backed fusible web

Black machine embroidery thread (30-weight)

White machine embroidery thread (30-weight)

Teal embroidery floss

Temporary fabric adhesive spray

Erasable fabric pen or pencil

TIP
Baby quilts can be fun and whimsical, even if you use an earthy color palette.

One, two, three, four, five,
Once I caught a fish alive,
Six, seven, eight, nine, ten,
Then I let go again.

Why did you let it go?
Because it bit my finger so.
Which finger did it bite?
This little finger on the right.

Linen:

Cut 1 piece 41″ × 44″
(104.1cm × 111.8cm) for quilt top.

Striped fabric:

Cut 5 strips 1″ (2.5cm) wide × width of
fabric for binding.

INSTRUCTIONS

*Seam allowances are ¼″ (6mm) unless other-
wise noted.*

1. Trace the appliqué templates for
Herring 1–3 from Silakka Pillow (pages
85–86) and Flounder (page 93), and
prepare the appliqué pieces following the
appliqué instructions on pages 17–20. Peel
off the paper from the appliqué pieces, and
pin them on the quilt top using the project
photo for reference.

2. Thread your sewing machine with
black embroidery thread, and appliqué the
fish. Note that the fin in the middle of
the flounder and the stripes on the tail fin
are part of the quilting and should not be
stitched yet at this point.

3. Compose the backing if you are putting it together from scraps. The backing
fabric and the batting should be about
1″ (2.5cm) larger than the quilt top
on all sides, approximately 43″ × 46″
(109.2cm × 116.8cm).

4. Stack and baste the quilt layers together (pages 22–23).

5. Draw 8 lines across the quilt, using an erasable fabric pen, starting about 7″ (17.8cm) from the top. Space the lines 5″ (13cm) apart. Then mark the first sentence from the rhyme using your own handwriting. Find tips on free-motion quilting on page 23.

6. Set your sewing machine for free-motion quilting, and quilt the first line. Then mark the second line of the rhyme, quilt, and continue until you have finished quilting the text.

7. Quilt the fin and tail on the flounder.

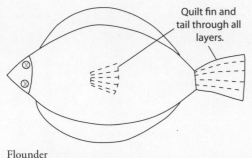

Quilt fin and tail through all layers.

Flounder

8. Thread your sewing machine with white embroidery thread. Stitch bubble shapes through the layers (see detail photo on page 92). Stitch a few times in place to secure the thread. I stitched a lot of bubbles around the fish and then made streams of bubbles over the quilt, leaving some areas unquilted to give it an organic feel.

9. Join the binding strips into a long strip, and bind the quilt using the single-fold binding technique (pages 24–25).

10. Wash the quilt.

11. Stitch the herring eyes with cross-stitch, using 4 strands of teal floss. I chose to make a visible knot and tassels on the back of the quilt. Cut 2 small rounds from white felt for the flounder eyes, and attach them with a cross-stitch (page 25).

12. One, two, three, four, five, your quilt is alive!

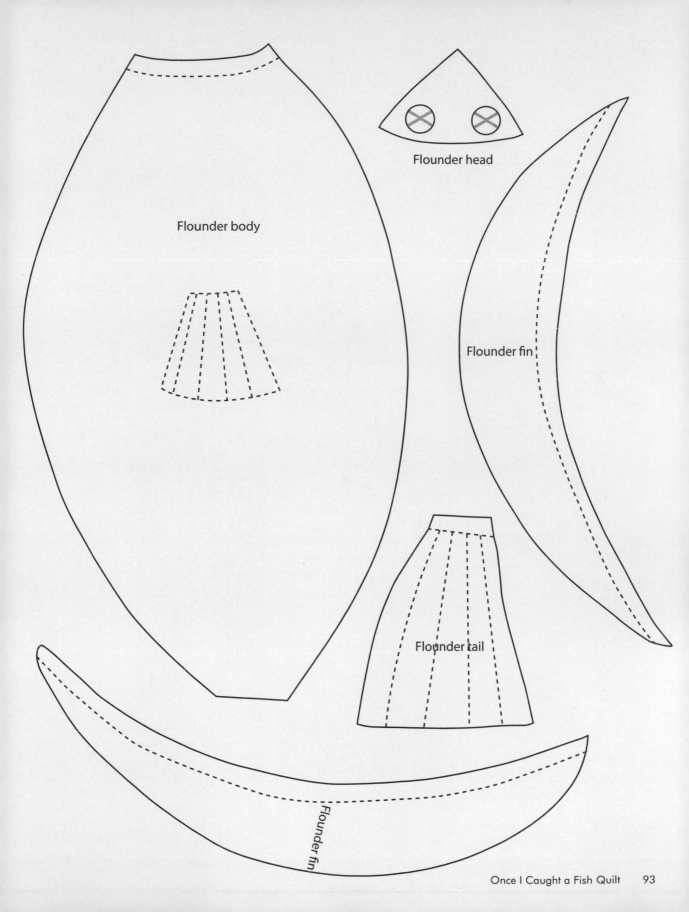

Flounder body

Flounder head

Flounder fin

Flounder tail

Flounder fin

autumn

stop to pick some flowers wallhanging

The air is soft but still warm, school has begun, and we're back to everyday life after the holidays. It's time to bring in the last flowers of summer and make it cozy inside.

This is an updated wallhanging that flirts with tradition. For this project, I found inspiration from traditional Scandinavian wool embroidery in which bright, naive figures are stitched onto a black background. I chose to sew on thin black linen and made my interpretation of the Swedish Dala horse.

Finished size:
17″ × 14¾″
(43.2cm × 37.5cm)

WHAT YOU'LL NEED

Fabrics

⅝ yard (60cm) of black linen or cotton for background

9″ × 9″ (23cm × 23cm) piece of natural linen or beige cotton for horse

Scrap of polka dot fabric for wagon

Fabric scraps for flowers, saddle, hitch, harness, and leaves

Notions and Supplies

¼ yard (25cm) of paper-backed fusible web

Black machine embroidery thread (30-weight)

White machine embroidery thread (30-weight)

Linen crochet yarn for mane and tail

Red embroidery floss

1 tiny button for eye

2 black buttons for wagon wheels

20″ (51cm) wooden stick for hanging

Erasable fabric marker or white chalk pencil

TIP

White thread against a black background creates an exciting effect that is reminiscent of chalk on a blackboard.

CUTTING

Black linen:

Cut 1 piece 18¼″ × 19″ (46.4cm × 48.3cm).

INSTRUCTIONS

1. Trace the appliqué pieces (patterns are on pages 100–101) onto the paper side of the fusible web, cut out, and fuse onto the fabric scraps. See pages 17–20 for more tips on fusible appliqué.

2. Peel off the paper from the prepared fabric pieces, and place onto the background in the numbered order using the Layout diagram (page 99) and the project photo for reference. Fuse the legs of the horse only at this point.

3. Machine stitch around the edges of the appliqué pieces with a straight stitch, using black embroidery thread, in the numbered order. Also stitch the dandelion, the mouth, and the horse shoes as shown in the Layout diagram.

4. Decorate the harness with cross-stitch (page 25), sewing by hand with 3 strands of red embroidery floss.

5. Now give the horse a mane and a tail. To make the mane, thread the needle with 2 strands of linen yarn, and sew with double thread. Tie in a knot from the right side of the project. Make the tail the same way; it should be around 2″ (5cm) long when finished. Fuse the entire horse to the linen, and machine stitch the edge with a straight stitch using black machine embroidery thread

6. Add buttons for the horse's eye and the wagon wheels.

7. Trace the text (pattern on page 100) with an erasable fabric marker or white chalk pencil.

8. Thread your sewing machine with white thread, and set the machine for free-motion stitching. See pages 20–21 for instructions. Stitch the text, and then press from the back side.

9. Fold the sides and the lower border ½" (1.3cm), and press. Fold another ½", and press. Topstitch with black thread.

10. To make the hanging channel on the upper border. Make a ½" (1.3cm) fold, and press. Then make a 2" (5cm) fold, press, and hand stitch along the bottom edge.

11. Place the stick in the hanging channel, and hang the piece on your wall!

Layout diagram

Enlarge script 150%

7
Flower

8
Flower
center

15
Leaf
Make 5.

14

12

13

11

9
Dandelion

10
Dandelion
center

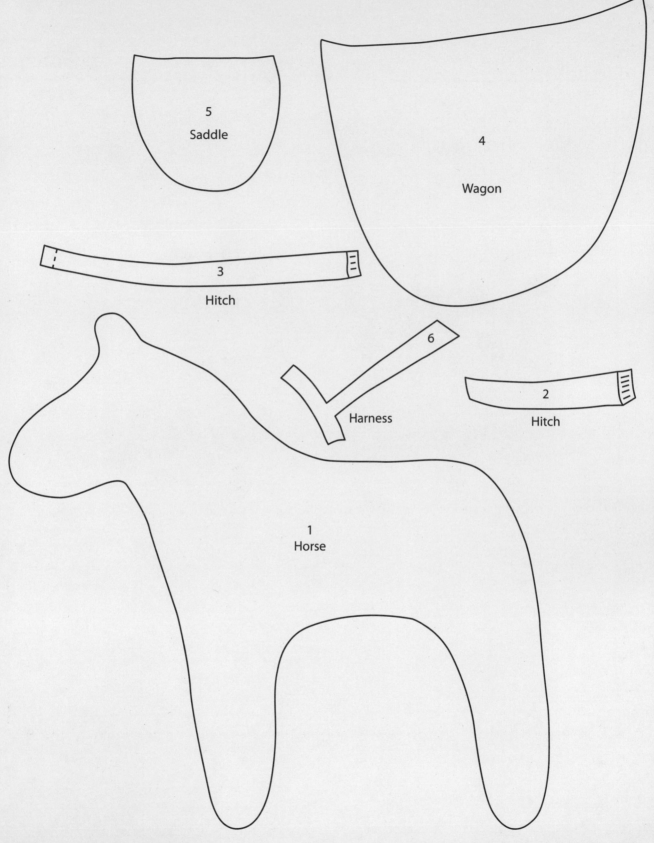

5
Saddle

4
Wagon

3
Hitch

6
Harness

2
Hitch

1
Horse

ruska quilt

Nature is on fire! Many people travel to the north this time of year to experience the symphony of colors we call *ruska*. On our way to school, we stop to jump in the piles of maple leaves. Inspired by all the beautiful shades of red, yellow, and green, I made a big version of my tree design.

Use the quilt as a cozy lap quilt on the sofa, or hang it on a wall.

Finished size:
52″ × 56″
(132cm × 142.2cm)

WHAT YOU'LL NEED

Fabrics

1¾ yards (1.6m) of natural-colored linen 55″ (140cm) wide for background

1¾ yards (1.6m) of print 55″ (140cm) wide for backing

¼ yard (25cm) of orange cotton for binding

Approximately 20 different fabric scraps of green, lime, brown, yellow, orange, burnt orange, and red polka dot for leaves

Notions

1¾ yards (1.6m) of cotton batting

½ yard (50cm) of paper-backed fusible web

Black machine embroidery thread (30-weight)

White machine embroidery thread (30-weight)

Erasable fabric pen or pencil

CUTTING

Linen:
Cut 52″ × 56″ (132cm × 142cm) rectangle for quilt top.

Backing and batting:
Cut 55″ × 60″ (140cm × 152.4cm) each of batting and backing.

Orange cotton:
Cut 6 strips 1″ (2.5cm) wide for the binding.

INSTRUCTIONS

Seam allowances are ¼" (6mm) unless otherwise noted.

1. Trace the appliqué template for the leaf below, and draw 52 leaves on the paper side of the fusible web. Cut out and press onto the leaf fabrics, making 1–4 leaves from each fabric.

2. Find a table or floor, and spread out your canvas—the background linen fabric. Place a blanket or a piece of fabric underneath that can withstand heat so you can fuse the leaves without moving the quilt.

3. Using the project photo for reference, place the leaves on the quilt. Use an erasable fabric pen or pencil to draw the outline of the tree as you go. The tree trunk should be about 15½" (39cm) long before the first branch starts on the right side. The distance between the leaves is around 1¾" (4.4cm). Move the leaves around until you are satisfied with the order, and then press to fuse them in place. Check the manufacturer's instructions for the erasable fabric pen; you may need to be careful not to press the pen marks, or they may be set permanently.

4. Stitch the tree trunk, and appliqué the leaves at the same time, following the drawn lines and using black embroidery thread. First stitch around the leaf, then sew back and forth to form the vein in the middle.

5. Press from the back side.

6. Stack and baste the quilt sandwich (pages 22–23).

7. Set your sewing machine for free-motion quilting. Start quilting leaf shapes with white thread, starting from the middle of the quilt. Leave the tree trunk unquilted. Stitch around the leaves to make them rise from the background.

8. Trim the edges of the batting and backing so they are even with the quilt top.

Leaf quilting

9. Join the binding strip to make 1 long strip, and press (pages 24–25). Attach to the quilt using the single-fold binding technique.

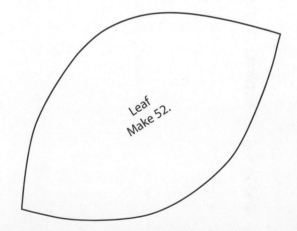

Leaf
Make 52.

autumn tree linen scarf

So many people like wearing black. Black does not have to be dull, especially when combined with lime green! Linen has a natural starch and shine that makes it ideal for garments.

You end up with a lot of small scraps doing fusible web appliqué. I like to save these for small projects. For the leaves on this scarf, I used scraps left over from the *Ruska Quilt* (page 102).

Finished size:
10″ × 63″
(25.4cm × 160cm)

WHAT YOU'LL NEED

Fabrics

¾ yard (70cm) of black linen for scarf

¾ yard (70cm) of lime green cotton with dots for lining

12 fabric scraps in fall colors for leaves

Scraps of polka dot and white fabric for toadstool

Notions

Lime green machine embroidery thread (30-weight)

Black sewing thread

Paper-backed fusible web

Erasable fabric pen or white chalk pencil

¼ yard (25cm) paper-backed fusible web

CUTTING

Black linen:
Cut 2 strips 10½″ (26.7cm) from the full width of black linen.

Lime lining fabric:
Cut 2 strips 10½″ (26.7cm) from the full width of lime lining fabric.

Toadstool cap

Toadstool stem

Seam allowances are ¼" (6mm) unless otherwise noted.

1. Join the 2 pieces of linen together end to end, press, and trim to 63½" (161cm) or the desired length. Repeat with the lining fabric to create a 10½" × 63½" (26.7cm × 161cm) piece.

2. Trace the toadstool patterns (page 106) onto the paper side of the fusible web. Cut out leaf shapes that are ½"–¾" (1.3cm–1.9cm) long from fabric scraps (with fusible web). Cut them freehand—they do not all need to be the exact same shape. You will need 38 leaves—3 or 4 leaves from each fabric.

3. Draw the tree trunk with an erasable fabric pen or white chalk pencil at one end of the linen. My tree is about 10" (25cm) high and about 7" (17.8cm) wide. Peel off the paper from the leaves, and arrange them using the project photo for reference. Fuse.

4. Stitch the tree and the leaves using lime green thread.

5. Make the toadstool appliqué at the other end of the scarf.

6. Pin the linen and the lining right sides together. Join together, leaving an opening at one end. Turn right side out, and press.

7. Close the opening by sewing a decorative stitch around the edges of the scarf.

sweet and sour apple coasters

It's harvest time, and the kitchen smells of homemade apple puree.
Making puree is worth the effort; having apples in the freezer during
wintertime is an everyday luxury.

This is a sweet and fun project for when you don't have much time.
The instructions are for a set of 4 coasters.

**Finished
size:** 4″ × 4″
(10.2cm × 10.2cm)

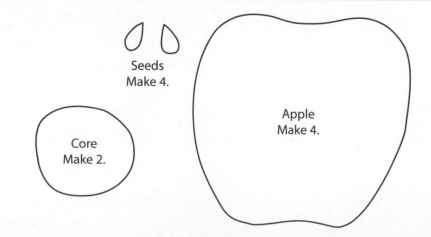

Seeds
Make 4.

Core
Make 2.

Apple
Make 4.

Fabrics

¼ yard (25cm) of natural-colored linen or cotton for backgrounds and backing

3 red pieces and 1 lime green piece of fabric 5″ × 5″ (13cm × 13cm) for apples

White and black scraps of fabric for apple cores and seeds

Notions

¼ yard (25cm) of low-loft batting

¼ yard (25cm) of paper-backed fusible web

Black machine embroidery thread (30-weight)

White machine quilting thread (30-weight)

Linen:

Cut 8 squares 4½″ × 4½″ (11.4cm × 11.4cm).

Batting:

Cut 4 squares 4½″ × 4½″ (11.4cm × 11.4cm).

Seam allowances are ¼″ (6mm) unless otherwise noted.

1. Trace the appliqué templates (page 108) onto the paper side of the fusible web. Prepare the appliqué pieces as described on pages 17–20. Peel off the paper on the back of the appliqué pieces. Position the pieces on 4 of the linen squares. See the project photo for reference. Press.

2. Thread the sewing machine with black embroidery thread. Sew carefully with a short straight stitch around the edges of each apple, using the appliqué foot on your sewing machine. Stitch the core and the seeds. Then set the sewing machine for a short and wide zigzag stitch to make the stems. Try out the stitches on a scrap first to be sure to get the stems you want!

3. Thread the machine with regular sewing thread. Place the batting pieces under the apple squares. Pin the appliquéd linen squares and the linen backing squares right sides together, and stitch ¼″ (6mm) from the edges, leaving an opening. Trim the corners. Turn the pieces right side out, and press.

4. Thread your sewing machine with white thread. Stitch close to the edges of the apples to quilt the coasters. Topstitch with a straight stitch using black thread close to the edges. This will close the openings.

Invite your friends to dinner!

*joy to the world

yule

merry mouse pouch with zipper

The counting of days has started, and I have prepared an Advent calendar with small gifts for the children. In one of the packages they will find a little mouse pouch, just big enough to collect small treasures.

Finished size:
6" × 7½"
(15.2cm × 19cm)

WHAT YOU'LL NEED

Fabrics

5" × 7" (13cm × 18cm) piece of striped green fabric for background

5" × 7" (13cm × 18cm) piece of red polka dot fabric for background

7" × 9" (18cm × 23cm) piece of red-and-white fabric for back

¼ yard (25cm) of fabric for lining

6" × 6" (15cm × 15cm) piece of light gray felt for head

Scrap of pink felt for ears

Scrap of red cotton for hat

Scrap of white polka dot cotton for dress

TIP
If you want an ecological option for felt, use a felted sweater!

Notions

6″ × 6″ (15cm × 15cm) paper-backed fusible web

8″ (20cm) of white cotton lace trim

5½″ (14cm) red zipper

Little bell for tomte hat

Black button for nose

Tiny black buttons for eyes

Black machine embroidery thread (30-weight)

CUTTING

Striped fabric: Cut 1 piece 6½″ × 4¼″ (16.5cm × 10.8cm).

Red Polka dot fabric: Cut 1 piece 6½″ × 4¼″ (16.5cm × 10.8cm).

Backing fabric: Cut 1 piece 6½″ × 8″ (16.5cm × 20.3cm).

Lining fabric: Cut 2 pieces 6½″ × 8″ (16.5cm × 20.3cm).

INSTRUCTIONS

Seam allowances are ¼″ (6mm) unless otherwise noted.

1. Trace the dress and the hat patterns (pages 115) onto the paper side of the fusible web, and prepare the appliqué pieces as described on pages 17–20.

2. Trace the head and ear patterns, and cut them out from the gray and pink felt. Do not use fusible web for the head and ears.

3. Join the green stripe and red polka dot front pieces together along their long edges, and press. Cover the seam with white lace, using a short straight stitch.

4. Place the appliqué pieces on the background. Peel off the paper on the back of the dress and the hat, and fuse into place. Pin the head and ears in place.

TIP

If you want the mouse to be less Christmassy, it can easily be made into a party mouse by choosing a different colorway and putting a little sequin on top of the hat. A lovely birthday gift for a child of any age!

5. Thread the sewing machine with black thread, and secure the appliqué with a short straight stitch. Start by stitching the hat, and continue as indicated in the Stitching diagram.

Stitching diagram

6. Cut off the loose ends, and give the mouse a pair of eyes, a nose, and a bell on the hat.

7. Now sew on the zipper, using the zipper foot on your sewing machine. Place the zipper right sides together with the top edge of the front piece. Pay attention to the seam allowances so that the zipper won't end up too close to the edge. Stitch the zipper to the front of the pouch. Then join the back piece right sides together with the other right side of the zipper.

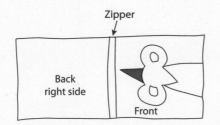

8. Place the right side of a lining piece along the wrong side of the zipper; the zipper remains in between. Stitch close to the zipper teeth. Repeat with the remaining lining piece, along the other half of the zipper.

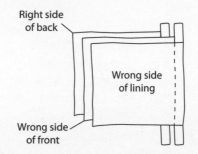

9. Press carefully from both sides, trying not to press the felt pieces. Make sure the fabric won't fold next to the zipper.

10. Pin the pouch right sides together, laying the front piece on top of the back piece and one lining piece on top of the other as shown in the illustration below. *Remember to leave the zipper open so you can turn the pouch right side out later.* Then sew the pouch together using a regular sewing foot. Start at the bottom of the lining.

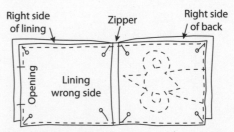

Pin right sides together and stitch around edges.

11. Trim the seam allowances and corners. Turn the pouch right side out, and stitch the gap closed. Push the lining inside the pouch.

TIP

If you use a heavier fabric for the pouch and a lightweight fabric for the lining, you might want to adjust the needle to make a smaller allowance for the outer part of the pouch. Otherwise you'll end up with a baggy-looking lining.

Hat
Make 1.

Ear
Make 2.

Head
Make 1.

Dress
Make 1.

Note: Patterns for hat and dress are reversed for fusible appliqué. Patterns for head and ears are not reversed.

tomte stuffy

The tomte, or tonttu, is the Scandinavian relative of Santa's little helper. During the month of December, these creatures will peek into our houses to see if the children are behaving well. This tomte is a product of my imagination. A mix of a tomte, an elf, and a garden gnome, he is a Christmas decoration—or, if treated well, a guardian of your home and family for the whole year.

Christmas fabrics from the 1960s and '70s have bold and bright patterns that might feel like a little bit too much today. This is a great place to give them a fresh new start!

Finished size:
approximately 24″ (61cm) from tip to toe

WHAT YOU'LL NEED

Fabrics

¼ yard (25cm) of solid red or green fabric for cap

¼ yard (25cm) of vintage cotton print for dress and arms

Scrap of cotton for legs

Scrap of off-white flannel for face

Scrap of felt for mittens

Notions

Tiny buttons or beads for eyes

Red embroidery floss for mouth

Stuffing

Yarn to knit scarf

Ribbons, buttons, and fabric scraps for embellishment

Santa's little vocabulary:

Finnish = Tonttu

Swedish = Tomte

Danish/Norwegian = Nisse

INSTRUCTIONS

Seam allowances are ¼" (6mm) unless otherwise noted.

1. Trace the pattern pieces (pages 120–121), and cut out the pieces from the fabrics of your choice.

2. Join together the arms and the felt mittens, right sides facing. Put the arm pieces right sides facing, and sew together using the illustration below for reference. Trim the edges, turn right side out, and fill with stuffing.

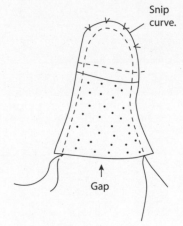

Snip curve.

Gap

Arm assembly

3. Sew together the legs, right sides facing. Trim the edges. Turn right side out, and stuff with stuffing.

4. Sew together the cap, the face, and the body, right sides facing. Do the same with the back piece. Press the seams toward the cap and dress sides.

5. If you want to add any embellishments to the dress, do it at this point. You can either stitch the face now or do it at the very end. Use 2 strands of embroidery floss for the mouth, and sew with a backstitch.

6. Stitch the arms and legs to the front dress piece as shown in the illustration below.

7. Pin the front and back pieces together, leaving an opening in one side (the legs will peek out of this opening—see the illustration below). Sew together carefully. Trim the edges, and turn right side out.

8. Stuff the tomte. You will need a lot off stuffing to get a steady cap and neck. Hand sew to close the gap.

9. Stitch the face if you did not do it earlier. Give your tomte a scarf and a name!

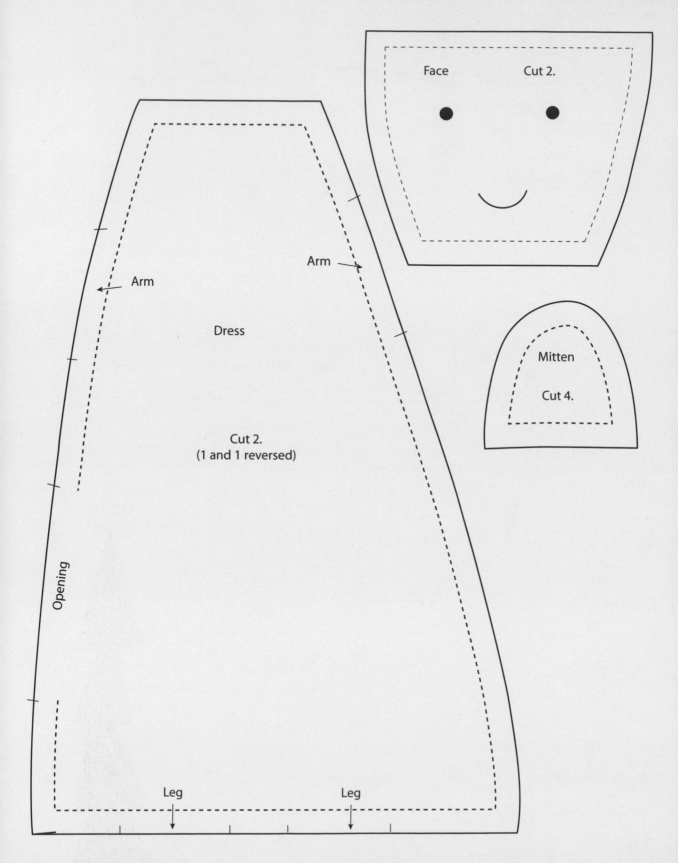

Face   Cut 2.

Arm

Arm

Dress

Cut 2.
(1 and 1 reversed)

Mitten

Cut 4.

Opening

Leg   Leg

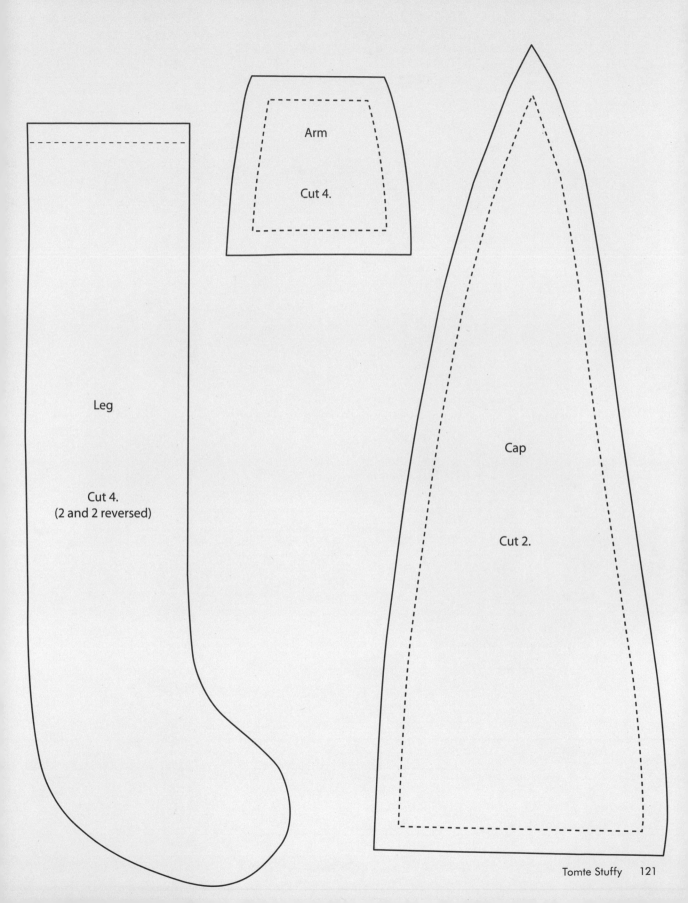

Arm

Cut 4.

Leg

Cut 4.
(2 and 2 reversed)

Cap

Cut 2.

yule house ornament

The weather in December is usually cold, windy, and wet, and I prefer to stay inside the house making gingerbread or sewing Christmas gifts.

These houses look fun in a row but can also be hung on a Christmas tree. One of my friends has hung hers on the front door to greet visitors. Personalize your house with your house number, buttons, and trim. On page 68, a house serves as a garden shed.

Finished size:
3″ × 7½″
(7.6cm × 19cm)

WHAT YOU'LL NEED

Fabrics

¼ yard (25cm) of print for house

5″ × 10″ (13cm × 25cm) piece of print for roof

Fabric scraps for door and window

Notions

Paper-backed fusible web

Black machine quilting thread

Button or sequin for doorknob

Trim for chimney

Stuffing

Ribbons, buttons, trim, and fabric scraps for embellishment

INSTRUCTIONS

Seam allowances are ¼″ (6mm) unless otherwise noted. Project patters are shown on page 125.

1. Trace the pattern piece for the roof. Cut out from 2 layers of fabric.

2. Cut 2 pieces 3½″ × 5″ (8.9cm × 12.7cm) for the house body.

3. Choose 1 of the patterns for a door and a window. Trace the window and door onto fusible web. Fuse onto fabric scraps, and cut out. Peel off the paper, and fuse into place using the project photos (pages 122 and 124) for reference.

4. Join the front roof and house pieces together, right sides facing. Press the seams toward the darker side. Repeat for the back pieces.

5. Appliqué the door and window using black thread.

6. Now embellish your house!

7. Fold a 3″ (7.6cm) piece of trim in half, and insert it along one edge of the roof to serve as a chimney. Stitch the house together along the edges, right sides facing, leaving an opening at the bottom.

In Finland, Yule is referred to as 'Joule' or 'Jul'

8. Turn the house right side out, and stuff with stuffing. Fold in the seam allowance at the bottom, and close the opening by hand or machine.

9. Add a hanging loop, and your house is ready to hang on the Christmas tree.

Roof

Cut 2.

Joulu

Jul

Window 1

Window 2

Window 3

24

Door 1

Door 2

fairy angel dolls

I call them fairy angels and like to make them nice and bright so they can spread joy all year long, instead of being packed away to collect dust with the seasonal decorations.

Finished size:
approximately 9″ (23cm) from tip to toe

Follow the sewing instructions and patterns for the Gardening Angel (pages 64–67) using the additional patterns below.

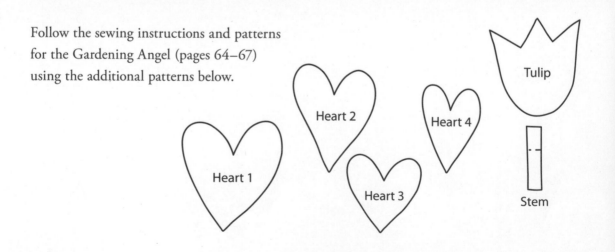

ABOUT THE AUTHOR

Kajsa Wikman is an artist, blogger, and teacher. She lives in Helsinki, Finland, with her family. She runs a small business, Syko Design, specializing in happy, childlike appliqué designs and printed products. Kajsa has previously contributed to the following books: *Quilts, Baby!* (Lark Books, 2009), *Pretty Little Pillows* (Lark Books, 2010), and *Whip Up Mini Quilts* (Chronicle Books, 2010).

Contact:
Website: www.syko.fi **Email:** info@syko.fi
Blog: syko.typepad.com **Phone:** +358 50 3602447
Shop: syko.etsy.com

ABOUT THE PHOTOGRAPHER

Sanna Peurakoski has ten years of experience as a professional photographer. She works in the fields of both commercial and fine art photography. In her work, she strives to reflect her personal motto: Beauty is the new punk.

RESOURCES

Michael Miller Fabrics, LLC
www.michaelmillerfabrics.com

Robert Kaufman Fabrics
www.robertkaufman.com

For a list of other fine books from C&T Publishing, ask for a free catalog:

C&T PUBLISHING, INC.
P.O. Box 1456
Lafayette, CA 94549
800-284-1114

Email: ctinfo@ctpub.com
Website: www.ctpub.com

C&T Publishing's professional photography services are now available to the public. Visit us at www.ctmediaservices.com.

Tips and Techniques can be found at www.ctpub.com > Consumer Resources > Quiltmaking Basics: Tips & Techniques for Quiltmaking & More

For quilting supplies:

COTTON PATCH
1025 Brown Ave.
Lafayette, CA 94549
Store: 925-284-1177
Mail order: 925-283-7883

Email: CottonPa@aol.com
Website: www.quiltusa.com

Note: Fabrics used in the quilts shown may not be currently available, as fabric manufacturers keep most fabrics in print for only a short time.